Praise for *Survi...*

"I am going to be starting session 9 n... week. So far it has been great. I combined sessions 1 and 2 and had students go through their own surveys and summarize it themselves. This was great because they could reflect on themselves. We had great discussions regarding this. Overall this has been a great program with wonderful information."

—**Sara Cox**, seventh grade science and math teacher,
South Meadow Middle School, Peterborough, NH

"I think this curriculum has helped students to identify what they do and feel and to give it a name. Students are starting to identify, on their own, goal supporting and goal defeating behavior. They explain how they can turn negative self-talk into positive self-talk and are starting to identify their stress and what they can do about it."

—**Paula Rounds**, fifth grade teacher, South Meadow Middle School,
Peterborough, NH

"Many of the activities have opened up discussion about stressors teens can experience. Even students that may not be verbally sharing are listening to the conversation. I believe it helps them to know that they are not the only ones experiencing these things."

—**Cindy Bradshaw**, South Meadow Middle School, Peterborough

"One very simple aspect of the Managing Stress curriculum that I like is the use of the word 'stress.' Kids and adults alike can relate to this word!"

—**Ben Nester**, school psychologist, South Meadow Middle School,
Peterborough, NH

"We have had much success with the 'Managing Stress' curriculum. Our students check in each morning and have been able to, over time, see the link between a good night of sleep, breakfast, talking about their stress, and having a good day. Many times, students will link their weekly goals to the areas on their morning check in that seem to be troublesome (going to bed at the same time each night, having breakfast or simply asking to stay with us during advisory). The learning and language allows us (adults) to assess student needs before they become so big that the kids get overwhelmed and shut down. They have all noted to us as well that they like to be able to talk about little things before they become bigger issues."

—**Sarah Milos**, Project ME program teacher,
West Running Brook Middle School Derry, NH

Surviving School Stress

Strategies for Well-Being in Today's Complex World

Marcel Lebrun and Eric Mann

ROWMAN & LITTLEFIELD
Lanham • Boulder • New York • London

Published by Rowman & Littlefield
A wholly owned subsidiary of The Rowman & Littlefield Publishing Group, Inc.
4501 Forbes Boulevard, Suite 200, Lanham, Maryland 20706
www.rowman.com

Unit A, Whitacre Mews, 26-34 Stannary Street, London SE11 4AB

British Library Cataloguing in Publication Information Available

Library of Congress Cataloging-in-Publication Data

Names: Lebrun, Marcel, 1957- author.
Title: Surviving school stress : strategies for well-being in today's complex world / Marcel Lebrun and Eric Mann.
Description: Lanham : Rowman & Littlefield, [2016] | Includes bibliographical references.
Identifiers: LCCN 2016039448 (print) | LCCN 2016039845 (ebook) | ISBN 9781475820478 (cloth : alk. paper) | ISBN 9781475820485 (pbk. : alk. paper) | ISBN 9781475820492 (Electronic)
Subjects: LCSH: Students—Mental health. | School mental health services. | Stress in children—Treatment. | Well-being.
Classification: LCC LB3430 .L45 2016 (print) | LCC LB3430 (ebook) | DDC 371.7/13—dc23
LC record available at https://lccn.loc.gov/2016039448

♾ ™ The paper used in this publication meets the minimum requirements of American National Standard for Information Sciences—Permanence of Paper for Printed Library Materials, ANSI/NISO Z39.48-1992.

Printed in the United States of America

Dedication from Marcel Lebrun

I dedicate this book to my husband Carl Daniels, who inspires and supports me throughout all of my adventures and endeavors.

The second dedication is to the thousands of students whom I have taught over the last thirty-six years of being an educator. I have seen what stress does to children, adolescents, teachers, and parents. The ravages of this phenomenon create destruction and unhappiness in too many. May the tools and strategies in this book make it better for all.

Dedication from Eric Mann

I dedicate Managing Stress for School Success *(Part 2 of this book) to my wife, daughters, friends, and colleagues who enrich my life every day by both adding to and alleviating my stress.*

Contents

Preface

Being at school has been a stressful experience for many students for over one hundred years. As the educational system became more student centered in the 1970s and 1980s, there seemed to be a new wave of stress that began to manifest. Students became empowered to take more of a role in their education, expectations were relaxed, curriculum became more experiential and teacher driven; all the while students began manifesting many external behavior problems and mental health issues started to rise.

The correlation though evident has been difficult to prove in terms of scientific research. Teachers and parents began to lose control. Sharp rises in school violence started to pop up throughout the country, standardized testing became the norm for accountability and responsibility, and stress became more of a focus.

According to the APA 2013 Stress in America Survey American teens today are the most stressed out age group of all the demographical groups. What has changed? What is causing this phenomenon? Is society to blame? Technology? Social media? Loss of parental and community values and clear expectations?

Children are coming to school with a wide variety of social and emotional issues. Teaching has been redefined and the job has become much more difficult to achieve the desired results as expected by state and national government educational systems. Students are manifesting problems in self-control, mood, or socializing impairments that are preventing successful learning and advancement.

Teachers are often asking themselves, "How can I teach a child with mental health issues when I don't have the skills?" "How do I deal with children with emotional and social problems and still do my job?" "What happens to all the healthy kids—I won't have time to teach them because of my focus on children with problems?" These concerns are echoed throughout the country and solutions must be presented in terms of training and resources.

When children and adolescents enter a school or a new developmental milestone (preschool, kindergarten, middle, or high school), they start feeling overwhelmed by the stressors in this environment. This crisis presents an opportunity for changes that are beneficial to the student's overall ability to cope. During a period of crisis, a person's normal defenses are down and emotional distress becomes high.

This person may feel an urgency to decrease the level of emotional distress. Because they are motivated toward alleviating emotional distress, they are open to new ways of thinking and behaving, often leading to escape or challenging behaviors (flight or fight) that alleviate the current stressor but may set the stage for increased stress down the road via social and academic consequences for the behaviors.

The responses to stress are numerous and so are the approaches for dealing with it. What works for one person may not work for another. Therefore, it is necessary to be prepared with a number of strategies for handling stress. It is a only a matter of taking time to investigate to see what is out there that may suit the purposes and implementing the necessary strategies to take control back in a way that is supportive of students and helps students build their capacity for emotional self-regulation.

The tasks of teaching and supporting children with issues related to anxiety, behavior, stress, and psychological impairments can be daunting and discouraging. This book will provide a wide variety of strategies, interventions, and a curriculum for regular and special educators to use in their efforts to better serve their clients as well as supporting the parents of these children.

Acknowledgments

I would like to thank Eric Mann who contributed his ideas for the curriculum on Managing Stress in the Classroom. His foresight in recognizing the need for an advisory curriculum will be an exceptional resource for teachers and educators to have at their disposal. His work and his contributions will make a difference for many students.

I would also like to thank my graduate assistant Melissa Clay for her help in the research and editing of this manuscript.

Part I

STRESS: BELIEFS, INFLUENCES, AND SOLUTIONS

Chapter 1

Types of Stress

Understanding stress can be overwhelming and confusing due to its myriad characteristics, symptoms, duration, and treatment approaches. In this chapter a summary is included of the major types of stress.

TYPE 1 ACUTE STRESS

Acute stress is the most common form of stress. It comes from demands and pressures of the recent past and anticipated demands and pressures of the near future. Some examples include students being in a school play, playing in a big game after school, competing in a personal or team challenge, or studying for placement tests to get a scholarship to get into an Ivy League college. By the same token, an overdose of short-term stress can lead to psychological distress, tension headaches, upset stomach and other symptoms (ACE Study 1997).

Acute stress symptoms are short term; acute stress doesn't have enough time to do the extensive damage associated with long-term stress. The most common symptoms are:

- Emotional distress—some combination of anger or irritability, anxiety and depression are the three stress emotions.
- Muscular problems including tension headache, back pain, jaw pain and the muscular tensions that lead to pulled muscles and tendon and ligament problems.
- Stomach, gut and bowel problems such as heartburn, acid stomach, flatulence, diarrhea, constipation and irritable bowel syndrome.

- Transient overarousal leads to elevation in blood pressure, rapid heartbeat, sweaty palms, heart palpitations, dizziness, migraine headaches, cold hands or feet, shortness of breath and chest pain.

(APA 2015)

Acute stress is highly treatable and manageable. This heightened stress is an important part of the development process that most children and adolescents experience. The variety of life experiences often become developmental milestones that empower the child or adolescent to test out their ever growing and developing physical and psychological systems. Only by being slightly stressed can they challenge themselves. Stress during psychological development challenges the student to seek out and achieve new levels of internal and external experiences that enable or foster a new maturity or intellectual development.

TYPE 2 EPISODIC ACUTE STRESS

The symptoms of episodic acute stress are the symptoms of extended overarousal: persistent tension headaches, migraines, hypertension, chest pain, and heart disease. Treating episodic acute stress requires intervention on a number of levels, generally requiring professional help, which may take many months (APA 2015).

These students seem to be overaroused, short-tempered, irritable, anxious, and tense. Some of these students may actually be mislabeled as having ADHD-like symptoms. Because of their lack of organizational skills or self-management coping skills they are always in a hurry, they tend to be abrupt, and sometimes their irritability comes across as hostility. Interpersonal relationships deteriorate rapidly because others cannot tolerate their outbursts, acting up, temper tantrums, and their need for control and power (Stress in America Survey 2011).

There are students that are excessive worriers. They worry about the test, the grades, how others perceive them socially, making the team, being chosen or recognized, school shootings, or being poisoned by school lunch, and are constantly on alert. Their sense of overarousal becomes their dominant coping mechanism. They see the potential for disasters everywhere. The level of agitation becomes marginally manageable. These students are more likely to become anxiety driven or depressed. Rarely do they become overly hostile, angry or dangerous (Stress in America Survey 2011).

Often, lifestyle and personality issues are so ingrained and habitual with these students that they do not know any other way of coping unless teachers, support professionals, and/or parents have made a consistent effort to teach them new ways of thinking or doing. These students, if old enough to understand the impact of their behaviors, blame their woes on other people and external events, such as my teacher hates me, or my parents won't let me do what I want.

They begin to see themselves as victims to the adults around them because they do not have the power to influence or change what they are living or enduring (Miller and Smith 1993). They can be fiercely resistant to change. Only the promise of relief from pain and discomfort of their symptoms can be the opening to receiving support and skill enhancement from their teachers or parents. This is where schools can play an important role in treatment.

The goal is to teach these children and adolescents what tolerable stress is, which we know is intense but can be a relatively short-lived experience. Usually this type of stress can be overcome with support/caring or become positive stress that leads to new energy sources that can be redirected and support new ways of thinking and acting.

TYPE 3 CHRONIC STRESS

While acute stress can be motivating to some, chronic stress is not. This is the grinding stress that wears students away day after day, year after year. Chronic stress destroys bodies, minds, and lives. It wreaks havoc through long-term attrition. It is the stress of poverty, of dysfunctional families, and of being trapped within a classroom that is unsafe, unsupportive, and toxic. It is the stress that the never-ending "troubles" have brought to fruition.

The lack of safety in a community, drugs, bullying and cyber-bulling, the presence of gangs and their warfare, maltreatment, and abuse (physical, emotional, sexual, and neglect) are but a few of the factors that play a role in the student's ability to be successful within a specific family, school, or community. Psychological and behavioral problems begin when a student is unable to see a way out of a miserable situation. The stress of unrelenting demands and pressures for seemingly interminable periods of time become unmanageable and the individual loses hope and gives up searching for solutions.

Some chronic stresses stem from traumatic, early childhood experiences that become internalized and remain forever painful and present. Some experiences profoundly affect personality. A view of the world, or a belief system, is created that causes unending stress for the individual (e.g., the world is a threatening place, people will find out you are a pretender, and you must be perfect at all times). This is when personality or deep-seated convictions and beliefs must be reformulated and recovery requires active self-examination, often with professional help (Miller and Smith 1993).

The worst aspect of chronic stress is that people get used to it. They forget it is there. People are immediately aware of acute stress because it is new; they ignore chronic stress because it is old, familiar, and sometimes, almost comfortable.

Chronic stress kills through suicide, violence, heart attack, stroke and, perhaps, even cancer (APA 2015). People wear down to a final, fatal breakdown. Because physical and mental resources are depleted through long-term attrition, the symptoms of chronic stress are difficult to treat and may require extended medical as well as behavioral treatment and stress management (APA 2015).

The ACE Study is ongoing collaborative research between the Centers for Disease Control and Prevention in Atlanta, Georgia, and Kaiser Permanente in San Diego, California. The co-principal investigators of the study are Robert F. Anda, MD, MS, with the CDC; and Vincent J. Felitti, MD, with Kaiser Permanente. Over seventeen thousand Kaiser Patients participating in routine health screening volunteered to participate in the study.

Data resulting from their participation continues to be analyzed; it reveals staggering proof of the health, social, and economic risks that result from childhood trauma. The following is a summary of some of their findings that are closely related to stress manifestation in students:

1. Almost two-thirds of participants reported childhood abuse, neglect, or exposure to other adverse experiences; more than one-fifth reported having experienced severe stress and difficulty coping with life issues and challenges.
2. The greater the number of adverse experiences, the greater the risk for health and behavioral outcomes such as alcoholism, drug use, smoking, depression, chronic obstructive pulmonary disease, fetal death, ischemic heart disease, liver disease, sexually transmitted diseases, multiple sexual partners, intimate partner violence, suicide attempts, and unplanned pregnancies.
3. Adverse childhood experiences are directly related to risky behaviors in childhood and adolescence.
4. As adverse childhood experiences increase, so do the number of co-occurring health conditions.
5. 25% of women and 16% of men reported experiencing child sexual abuse and were more than twice as likely to report suicide attempts.
6. A strong relationship was found between physical abuse, sexual abuse, and witnessing of intimate partner violence as a child and a male's risk of involvement with a teenage pregnancy.
7. Women who reported experiencing four or more types of abuse during their childhood were 1.5 times more likely to have an unintended pregnancy at or before the age of twenty.

8. Exposure to physical and sexual abuse and intimate partner violence in childhood resulted in women being 3.5 times more likely to report domestic abuse victimization, and men 3.8 times more likely to report intimate partner violence perpetration.
9. Participants with higher adverse childhood experiences were at greater risk of alcoholism, marrying an alcoholic, initiating drug use, and experiencing addiction; more likely to have thirty or more sexual partners and engage in sexual intercourse earlier; and have a higher probability of both lifetime and recent depression disorders.

(ACE Study, CDC 2015)

There is no doubt from the several examples mentioned above that life experiences do dictate future direction and the ability to have a successful life. Success is being defined as emotional, physical, and cognitive happiness.

COMMON CONTRIBUTORS TO STRESS

1. Time Stress
2. Anticipatory Stress
3. Situational Stress
4. Encounter Stress

(Albrecht 2015)

Time Stress is when an individual worries about time, the lack of time, the number of things that have to be done, or the fear that one will fail to achieve something important. The student with time stress may feel trapped, unhappy, or even hopeless (Albrecht 2015).

Anticipatory stress describes stress that a student experiences concerning the future. Sometimes this stress can be focused on a specific event, such as a project, presentation, event, a big game, etc. Anticipatory stress can also be vague and undefined, such as an overall sense of dread about the future or a worry that something will go wrong. Children with anxiety disorders are great at manifesting this type of stress. The "What if" syndrome is prevalent and part of their thinking and behavioral patterns (Albrecht 2015).

Situational stress occurs when a student is in a situation in which they have no control. This could be during an emergency; however, most often it is a situation that involves conflict or a loss of some sort; concern about acceptance by a social group, friends, or teachers; or making a mistake in front of a group of peers (Albrecht 2015).

Encounter stress revolves around people. Students experience stress when they worry about interacting with a certain group of students, a teacher, the principal, etc. The student may not like these individuals and is unsure how they will interact or react toward them. Students begin to feel stress when they are forced to interact with people that they perceive as being difficult or hostile. Sometimes encounter stress occurs in groups of children that have been together for extended periods of time or have been forced to interact with one to two children repeatedly.

PREVALENCE

The annual Stress in America Survey which was conducted online by Harris Interactive on behalf of APA among 1,226 residents in August and September 2011 and between August 3–31, 2013 showed that a large percentage of Americans consistently report high levels of stress (22 percent reported extreme stress). Americans continue to report 39 to 44 percent that their stress has increased over the last five years. This data makes the case that stress is a universal issue, one that should be addressed for all students as opposed to those who show apparent stress-related symptoms.

Teens report that their stress level during the school year far exceeds what they believe to be healthy (5.8 stress vs. 3.9 being healthy on a 10-point scale) and tops adults average reported stress levels (5.8 for teens vs. 5.1 for adults). Even during the summer, teens report their stress to be at an unhealthy level. Many teens also report feeling overwhelmed (31 percent) and depressed or sad (30 percent) as a result of stress. More than one-third of teens report fatigue or feeling tired (36 percent) and nearly 23 percent report skipping a meal because of stress (Stress in America Study 2013).

Despite the impact stress has on adolescents, teens are more likely to report (54 percent) that stress has a slight or no impact on their body or physical health than adults (39 percent). Adolescents believe (52 percent) that stress has little to no impact on their mental health versus 43 percent of adults (Stress in America Study 2013).

Norman B. Anderson stated, "It is alarming that the teen stress experience is so similar to that of adults. It is even more concerning that they seem to underestimate the potential impact that stress has on their physical and mental health. In order to break this cycle of stress and unhealthy behaviors as a nation, we need to provide teens with better support and health education at school and home, at the community level, and in their interactions with health care professionals" (Gegoire 2014).

Teens' habits around sleep, exercise, and technology (the average teen consumes an average of 7.5 hours of media per day) may play a role in contributing to higher stress levels (Masujah 2013). Today's teens spend time watching TV, listening to music, surfing the Web, social networking, and playing video games, according to a 2010 study of eight- to eighteen-year-olds conducted by the Kaiser Family Foundation. The study also found a particular rise in time spent on mobile devices: an overall increase of about an hour and twenty minutes since 1999 (Masujah 2013).

According to the Bureau of Labor Statistics' 2011 American Time Use Survey, high school students spent on average less than an hour per weekday on sports, exercise, and recreation. The lack of physical exercise has resulted in a variety of health-related problems for children and adolescents (obesity, eating problems, stress management). This generation of digital natives or Facebook generation is the first group to be overly involved with technology.

More than one in three teens say that stress has kept them up at night. The 2011 American Time Use Survey found that most teens aren't sleeping enough to begin with: the average teen sleeps 7.4 hours each school night—far less than the recommended 9–10 hours. The survey also found that one in five teen's reports exercising less than once a week or not at all, despite the proven stress-relieving benefits of physical activity.

Few teens (16 percent) in the annual Stress in America 2013 survey reported that their stress was on the decline. In contrast 31 percent believed their stress increased in the last year, while 34 percent believed their stress will increase in the coming year. Nearly 42 percent reported that they were doing very little to manage their stress and more than 13 percent never set aside time to manage stress. These results definitely indicate a pathway to increased stress, health issues, and long-range dysfunctional lifestyles or lack of development of coping strategies as adults.

The Harris Survey 2012, Missing the Health Care Connection demonstrated that Americans appear to be caught in a vicious cycle where they manage stress in unhealthy ways, and lack of willpower and time constraints impede their ability to make lifestyle or behavioral changes. There is also a troublesome trend emerging among families in which parents are underestimating how much stress their children experience and the impact their own stress has on their children.

Children as young as eight are reporting physical and emotional problems because of stress, child mental health is a significant public health problem. Children with psychopathology are less likely to complete schooling, are more dependent on government welfare programs, and have a greater risk of suicide and entering the criminal justice system (National Center for Health Statistics 2007).

STRESSORS

Definition: Stressors are the external demands of life or internal attitudes and thoughts that require us to adapt. Some stressors come from both sources.

List of stressors:

1. Emotional—relationship, damage to property, disappointment, rejection, sudden illness.
2. Family—break-up, death, new addition, accident, abuse, addictions, illness.
3. Social—drugs, alcohol, change in social status, marriage, finances.
4. Change—move, transitions, death of parent.
5. Chemical—substance abuse, food poisoning, toxins, bug bites (Lyme).
6. Work—lay offs, reduced hours, bad supervisors, harassment.
7. Decision—buying a new house, marriage, separation, new school, leaving home.
8. Phobic—claustrophobia, insects, snakes, elevators, flying, heights, driving, animals.
9. Commuting—traffic, weather, road rage, conditions.
10. Physical—illness, weight loss–gain, colds, flu, having a baby.
11. Disease—isolation, mortality, missing school, loss of income, family history (cancer).
12. Pain, loss of bodily functions, parental issues, loss of employment, suicide.
13. Environmental noise pollution, air pollution, move to city or rural, climate, over population, cultural, geographical.

Many of these stressors play a significant role in a student's ability to be goal-supporting or self-destructive through their thinking and actions. The ability of these students to access a level of skill or experience to manage stress successfully is unlikely if not provided with the correct resources or support.

MODEL OF STRESS (LEBRUN 2015)

The following model is a quick reference as to how stress begins and develops over time that eventually leads to problems with health, emotional and physical turmoil, and finally illness.

The external demands and pressures begin to impact a student once stress has been launched. A student's perceptions, past experiences, attitudes, beliefs, and values are all thrown into the mix of the student's life. Stress, depending on vulnerability factors will either take root and grow or will dissipate because student has the abilities to cope with the external demands and pressures. In more cases than not the child does not have the abilities or cognitive level to shift or question their thinking or paradigms.

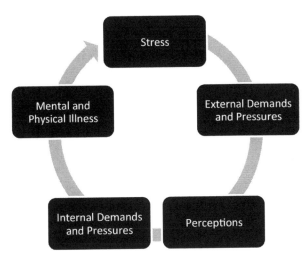

Figure 1.1   Stress Model. *Source*: M. Lebrun, 2015.

The vulnerability factors that are present in the child's experience to date become major players in the ability to manage the stressors. The vulnerability factors such as genetic disposition, coping skills, poor morale, impaired decision making, interpersonal reactions and interactions, absenteeism, money, poverty, abuse, poor executive functioning skills, etc., all have a role to play as to whether the child or adolescent is able to process the stress in a way that can lead to resolution.

For many children and adolescents perceptions begin to build an internal chaos or demand and the pressure builds. The child begins to formulate a list of responsibilities and has a perceived sense of obligation to someone (parent, teacher, siblings) and the stress builds (Pearlin et al. 1981).

As stress grows the ability to use executive skills is compromised. Formula: Stimulus-Executive skills-response + Stress (Mann and Bolick 2015). Once the stress begins, depending on the child's ability to seek support or to understand that they need support, a physiological and psychological breakdown begins and the student turns to unhealthy solutions: impulsivity (acting without thinking), self-criticism, substance abuse, self-inflicted harm.

The results are that a variety of symptoms, lack of sleep, poor nutrition, increased smoking, increased drug use, etc. all lead to development of an illness that could have been prevented with the right supports, stress management intervention, and strategies (Pearlin et al. 1981).

Stress can be difficult to understand. The habits, attitudes, and signs that can alert us to problems may be hard to recognize because they have become so familiar. Find your stress level right now by completing this test.

The Canadian Mental Health Association has designed a stress index test that is available at www.cmha.ca/mental_health/whats-your-stress-index/#. VMf0oi79x6I. It is scored immediately and provides great feedback to begin the discussion around what is causing stress and presents some solutions.

Chapter 2

Anxiety Disorders and Neurobiology of Stress

Teachers possess the power to create conditions that can help students learn a great deal, or keep them from learning much at all. Teaching is the intentional act of creating those conditions, and good teaching requires that we understand the inner sources of both the intent and the act.

Parker Palmer (2000)

Students with anxiety disorders experience irrational, excessive, and sometimes insurmountable amounts of anxiety that lead to a crippling amount of stress. Anxiety disorders are very rarely short lived and can last extended periods of time or even a lifetime. Anxiety affects a child's ability to learn, interact, and feel successful or productive in a school or community environment.

The most common anxiety disorders are Generalized Anxiety Disorder (GAD), Obsessive-Compulsive Disorder (OCD), Social Anxiety Disorder, Post-Traumatic Stress Disorder (PTSD), Panic Disorder, and School Refusal (APA 2015).

Understanding the neurobiology of stress is critical to understanding the causes and characteristics of these disorders. In the last ten years, much progress has been made in understanding the causes of stress as well as the role that the brain plays in the development, maintenance, and recovery of stress.

NEUROBIOLOGY OF STRESS

The amygdala is part of the brain's limbic system, which is involved in the modulation and expression of emotions. External stimuli are perceived through our sensory organs; information that we see, hear, touch, or smell is transmitted through neural connections to the amygdala. The amygdala integrates this sensory information for storage in and retrieval from memory. It also attaches emotional valence to the sensory information and then transmits this information to the other systems involved in the stress response. The amygdala is also neurally connected to the medial prefrontal cortex. This area of the brain is involved in planned behaviors, working memory, motivation, and distinguishing between internally versus externally derived models of the world (Knight et al. 1995).

In recent years there has been a growing focus on the influence of executive functioning skills and the role these skills play in the creation, development, or management of stress. Below is an organizational chart that outlines the specifics skills and the necessary components needed for effective management.

Scientific research on the brain has allowed educators and medical personnel to understand the scope of brain function. Here is a list of symptoms that are caused by the brain reaction in order of prevalence: irritability/anger; fatigue; lack of interest, motivation, or energy; feeling nervous/anxious; headache; feeling depressed or sad; feeling like crying; upset stomach; muscle tension; change in appetite; teeth grinding; change in sex drive; tightness in

Executive Skills Definitions

(Adapted by Mann, 2014 from *Peg Dawson, Center for Learning and Attention Disorders, Portsmouth, NH*)

Executive Skill:	Definition:
Organization	The ability to create and maintain well-ordered systems to keep track of information or materials.
Time Management	The ability to estimate how much time one needs to complete a task, and then stay within time limits and deadlines.
Planning and Prioritizing	The ability to create a sensible roadmap to reach a goal or to complete a task. This skill includes the ability to determine what is more and less important to focus on.
Mental Flexibility	The ability to revise plans in the face of obstacles, setbacks, new information or mistakes. It includes the ability to adapt/adjust to changing or unexpected conditions.
Response Inhibition	The ability to inhibit inappropriate or irrelevant responses or reactions to stimuli.
Thoughtful Decision-Making	As opposed to impulsive, spontaneous decision-making, thoughtful decision-making means that a thinking process is utilized to make every day decisions. The thinking process, if most effective, incorporates consideration of positive and negative immediate, short and long-term consequences from possible choices.
Task Initiation	The ability to begin tasks without too much procrastination in an efficient or timely fashion.
Sustaining Attention	The ability to maintain attention to a situation or task despite distractibility, fatigue, disinterest or boredom.
Working Memory:	Working memory is a type of memory used to hold information in our mind as we work on it. If working memory skills are weak for a student, he/she may struggle to manage (remember) some aspect of needed information The more information given or requested, the more working memory skills are needed to successfully complete the task.
Goal-Directed Persistence	The capacity to have a goal and follow through to the completion of the goal without being distracted by competing interests.
Emotional Control/Regulation	Emotion regulation refers to the ability to use and respond to emotions in a healthy manner.
Self-understanding or Metacognition	The ability to assess how well you understand yourself and to observe how you do things. A person with self-understanding has the ability to stand back and take a birds-eye view of oneself in a situation. It includes the ability to observe how you solve problems, how you monitor your behavior and how you evaluate your actions and choices.

Figure 2.1   **Executive Skills Definitions.** *Source*: Dawson, 2014.

chest; and feeling faint/dizzy (Vaalamo et al. 2002). The above are clearly measurable as compared to somatic complaints.

Somatic complaints are physical symptoms with no identifiable, specific physiological cause. Common pediatric somatic complaints include headaches, nausea, or abdominal pain. Nonspecific causes usually include psychological distress, anxiety, family patterns, and life events (Chapman 2009).

Somatic complaints may result in a vicious cycle wherein the physical symptoms lead to emotional stress, which further exacerbates the somatic symptoms. Prevalence rates have been estimated at 20 percent, increasing to 40 percent if children are ten years old or younger, and 55 percent at eleven to fifteen years old (Vaalamo et al. 2002).

Diagnosis

Diagnosis of anxiety is traditionally aided by the widely used Child Behavior Checklist (CBCL) (Achenbach 1991). Other scales that can be used for diagnosis and classification are the Multidimensional Anxiety Scale for Children (MASC), the Revised Children's Manifest Anxiety Scale (RCMAS) and the State-Trait Anxiety Inventory for Children (STAIC) (Maruish 2004).

In a meta-analysis of the RCMAS, STAIC, and CBCL, Seligman and Petersen (2004) found that all were comparably effective for differentiating children with an anxiety disorder to children without an anxiety disorder. However, they found these tools are not as effective in differentiating between anxiety disorder and another psychological disorder (Ibid.). In addition, Seligman and Petersen (2004) advised that for clinicians, these tools only be used as part of the comprehensive assessment in addition to diagnostic interviewing.

The MASC is a newer scale that includes four dimensions of childhood anxiety: physical symptoms, social anxiety, separation anxiety, and harm avoidance (Muris et al. 2002). It has been shown to be effective and reliable, but again for clinicians is only part of a comprehensive diagnostic assessment (Muris et al. 2002). The Behavior Assessment System for Children (BASC) scale has also been used with success.

Generalized Anxiety Disorder (GAD) is often found in students who have unrealistic fears about everyday activities. These students seem to do well in their endeavors and at school. The key word is *seems*. They may have exaggerated concerns about their schoolwork, leading to tension, self-consciousness, and/or frequent headaches that do not seem to have a physical root but a psychological or emotional cause (Mash and Wolfe 2002).

Children with GAD seem to worry about anything and everything. The "everything" list may include sports, health, schedules, friends, parents, appearance, weight, performance—name it and there is a kid with GAD who worries about it. Many of these worries are truly unfounded. Depending on the level of anxiety, they may suffer from excessive bouts of anxiety, which are an overreaction to a real-life event.

For example, a new teacher replaces their classroom teacher, the year-end school concert, transitioning to the middle or high school, which are all natural occurrences in a student's school life become stress-causing incidents that act as a trigger for an array of stress levels and behavioral manifestations.

A word of caution about these students: they are often difficult to spot within the classroom, as they are often well-behaved students or those that suffer in silence. The following are a list of behavior and symptoms to look for:

1. Express apprehension about tests, assignments, and grades.
2. Feel fatigued or restless.
3. Have trouble concentrating.
4. Overly emotional.
5. Experience frequent headaches, stomachaches, and other pains.
6. Avoid participating in school activities.
7. Absent frequently.
8. Misuse alcohol and drugs.

(Mash and Wolfe 2002)

CASE STUDY: MARILYN, SECOND GRADE (SEVEN YEARS OLD)

I had been teaching for over fifteen years when I encountered Marilyn, in second grade. Being a male teacher, she immediately was frightened of me upon entering on September 1, the first day of school. She began to cry, twirl, and twist her braid, refused to come near me, and would not do any work for me at all. This was all new for me as a teacher, as I was almost always successful with my students. This whining, crying, and refusal to participate went on for three days. I called the parents and we met and discussed the situation.

Marilyn was so anxious about school that it was a fight to get to school every morning. She could not sleep, was overly tired, and became sick. Finally the parents kept her home from school and took her to see their family doctor, a woman who was able to find the source of the anxiety. It turned out her older brother had told Marilyn that all male teachers were abusive and that I would abuse her as soon as we were alone. He had frightened her so much that her level of anxiety was over the top.

The parents, Marilyn, school counselor, principal, and I met and worked out a plan for success. Within a week, Marilyn was an active second grader doing all the activities that we did in second grade. She had an excellent year. If the team had removed her from my classroom, the anxiety of having a male teacher would have been reinforced and the problem delayed till she encountered her next male teacher. I am happy to report that once the anxiety was dealt with through professional help of the team, Marilyn continued to be successful (Lebrun 2000).

Students with Obsessive-Compulsive Disorder (OCD) often experience unwanted, intrusive thoughts or images (obsessions) which cause them to engage in repetitive behaviors (compulsions). One must understand that these obsessions and compulsions are very time consuming, interfere with school, routines, and will affect their performance on a variety of tasks, especially tasks that are timed or need completion within a period of time. It is reported that between 1 and 3 percent of children have OCD (APA 2015).

Obsessions take root in the mind when a child has a persistent thought that elicits anxiety, for example, "I have germs on my hands." These exaggerated thoughts or images begin to create a level of chaos in the child's thinking patterns and the child begins to worry excessively. The thoughts create a fear (contamination), and because the child is unable to get rid of the images or fears, the behavior then turns to a compulsion—a child who persistently thinks that their hands have germs on them may be washing them fifteen times a day, and wiping every surface touched by others with sanitizer and cleanser.

This compulsive behavior is the only way the child seems able to quiet the thoughts and anxiety for the moment. OCD is the exaggerated version of what happens when poorly managed stress leads the individual to behaviors that gain short-term relief at the cost of creating long-term problems. Some children with OCD do not have a specific fear but may feel as if things aren't right and will engage in compulsions till they believe they have solved or regulated the problem to their satisfaction. Unfortunately with OCD, the obsessive thoughts return and the cycle repeats.

Common obsessions and compulsions as listed by the American Psychological Association include the following:

Obsessions:
1. Fear of illness, death, or contamination.
2. Fear or image of harm to oneself or others.
3. Fear of doing or saying something evil or sinful.
4. Fear that something bad might happen: if something is not done correctly, in association with particular numbers, if something important is thrown away, if something is asymmetrical or out of order.

Compulsions:
1. Avoidance of germs or dirt (including excessive hand washing or showering).
2. Repeated requests for reassurance.
3. Frequent prayer or confessions.

4. Repeated checking of locks or appliances.
5. Extreme perfectionism.
6. Seeking balance by ordering, straightening, or arranging objects.
7. Doing activities in certain sets of numbers.
8. Excessive collecting or hoarding items of no value.

(APA 2015)

Behaviors and symptoms to look for in the classroom may be at times quite obvious like the compulsions, as those behaviors will often interfere with the classroom routines and procedures. The obsessions may be less obvious because it is tough to read the student's mind and therefore more difficult to measure or observe. There are milder neurotic versions of all these compulsions that impact a far greater percentage of the population than OCD. There is a difference between some milder neurotic obsessions and the ones that reach a higher level of pathology.

Classroom teachers are encouraged to look for the following behaviors and symptoms within their classroom or when working with children individually or small groups.

1. Child is indecisive and slow to accomplish task.
2. Child avoids some of the classroom materials.
3. Child washes hands excessively.
4. Child is stubborn, argumentative, and demanding.
5. Child acts in a distracted or an inattentive way.
6. Child repeats particular sounds, words, or music.
7. Child excessively requests assurance or explanations.
8. Child becomes irritable or has erratic mood swings.
9. Child is ostracized by peers.

(Mash and Wolfe 2002)

A newly defined disorder, Trichotillomania causes students to compulsively pull hair from their scalp, eyebrows, and eyelashes. The pulling relieves the tension from the anxiety and stress. Between 1 and 4 percent of people have this disorder; one-half of them show symptoms before age thirteen. Many more girls than boys are affected (Mansueto et al. 2001). If identified, referral to professional or medical doctor is highly encouraged.

CASE STUDY: PATRICK, FIFTH GRADE

As a middle school teacher I taught fifth grade for eight years because I loved this age group; they were both cool, yet young and impressionable.

Half way through the year Patrick began to walk around the class in circles and he would stop and touch certain parts of the walls at designated stops. This seemed to occur every day at the same time, around 2:40 pm.

At first as a classroom teacher I did not notice, as I had twenty-eight other students. He would do his rounds, count his textbooks, and line them up on his desk by color and size, followed by organization of all his pencils and pens in a very specific order. This became a problem when I was still teaching content, and he began his routine. Classes finished at 3 pm. Finally it came down to a showdown in the classroom because he started his routine during a test, and the other students became very agitated with him and what he was doing.

I pulled him out of class and wanted an explanation. He told me that he was anxious about getting on the bus and going home, so he needed to do this routine to stay calm and focused. In consultation with the parents, they too had noticed that at home he was manifesting behaviors that were typical of OCD. The family decided to address the situation with Cognitive Behavior Therapy and medications in conjunction with their doctor.

The only days Patrick demonstrated the OCD behaviors were whenever there was a substitute in my class or the routine of the day had been changed, or if there was an event that was very stressful. We were able to keep these triggers to a minimum and Patrick was successful in managing his symptoms 70 to 75 percent of the time (Lebrun 1997).

Social Anxiety Disorder affects students in social or performance settings. Students with this disorder may be excessively shy and hesitant or fear situations where they need to perform, answer a question publicly, or give a presentation or anything that has the potential for embarrassment or humiliation. This disorder often goes unrecognized and untreated. Many students keep this anxiety to themselves and are identified as just being shy. However, some children become so anxious they completely stop talking in public (Selective Mutism) and will only speak to their immediate families (Mash and Wolfe 2002).

The following are behaviors and symptoms to look for:

1. Acting in extremely shy manner.
2. Avoiding participating in school activities.
3. Acting in a distracted or confused way.
4. Being overly emotional.
5. Experiencing frequent headaches, stomachaches, and other physical pains.
6. Frequently missing school.

(Mash and Wolfe 2002)

A word of caution about working with children with Social Anxiety Disorder: some professionals or parents believe forcing a socially anxious child to interact with others will help them beat the anxiety. This does not respect the fear or the situation the child is in and may add more conflict, chaos, or mental anguish for the child because the parent or adult is not taking this disorder seriously.

Panic Disorder: between 1 percent and 5 percent of adolescents experience Panic Disorder. About one-half of these young people also experience another anxiety disorder or depressive disorder (Mash and Wolfe 2002). Within Panic Disorder classification, panic attacks are the most prevalent. A panic attack is a brief period of sudden, intense fear or discomfort that includes physical symptoms like chest pain, nausea, sweatiness, and dizziness, as well as feelings of unreality or doom. Panic disorders may cause children to avoid certain places, activities, or objects they fear will cause another episode.

Panic attacks are best explained by the fight or flight syndrome that we all have when we are in a difficult or in a highly arousing or over stimulating situation. This flight or fight reaction is caused by adrenalin and other chemicals that flood the body in a normal stress response that is meant to protect us. Adolescent students might experience this flight-fight in response to hormonal changes rather than real danger.

The effects might completely shut down the adolescent's capability to interact with others (Social Anxiety Disorder), or they might develop OCD, or a condition called agoraphobia where they are unable to escape or get help when panic occurs.

Behaviors and Symptoms to look for:

1. Visible physical changes (sweating, shaking, shortness of breath, dizziness).
2. Private, invisible sensations (heart palpitations, chocking, nausea, going crazy, dying).
3. Avoidance of certain places, activities, and people.
4. Inattention, very distracted, unable to remember details.
5. Slow, inadequate work production, constant self-monitoring, failure to finish tests.
6. Abuse of alcohol and drugs, student calming themselves with chemicals.

(Mash and Wolfe 2002)

Panic attacks are often fueled by unrealistic thinking and fears of the unknown while panic is always set off by specific situations, all potential stressors listed earlier, and could serve as possible triggers and therefore be part of the discussion when determining interventions.

School Refusal Anxiety Disorder (SRAD): this disorder is not a mental-health disorder. It refers to a student's fear or unwillingness to attend school. The most obvious sign is that a student is frequently absent from school. The reasons for a child not wanting to go to school are many and very varied.

Some of these children may have separation anxiety or social anxiety so they do not want to separate from their parents or are afraid of new situations.

These children have anxiety about their school performance. They may fear not being able to meet the classroom expectations, the guidelines on a project, the passing of a test or exam (test anxiety), or compete with their peers. Other compounding factors may be a student's fear for their safety and well-being.

Between 1 percent and 5 percent of children and adolescents refuse to attend school at some point. Ultimately about 10 percent of students over the age of sixteen drop out of school permanently (Fremont 2003). School attendance is significantly affected by experiences of bullying, teasing, and being ostracized by their peers.

Students who suffer from SRD experience difficulties at home and are concerned about family members or situations at home and worry excessively while at school. This situation is seen with some regularity when a sibling or parent is experiencing an illness. The child is afraid that the family member will die or get sicker if they are not there to monitor the situation.

Students who are disengaged and/or defiant just don't like school. They do not see the relevance of going to school, the work they are asked to do, or the value of education overall. Many would rather sleep till noon, play video games, and watch TV. They usually have had limited success or an overabundance of failure and punishment while at school and therefore have let go of any possible motivation to attend or continue in their education. This is really all about short-term relief and long-term cost. In earlier discussion the connection to executive skills development is paramount in the identification and management process.

Separation Anxiety Disorder is one of the most common causes of school refusal. This disorder is mostly seen (approximately 4 percent) in younger children entering preschool or kindergarten. Common signs are crying, tantrums, clinging behavior, stomachaches, headaches, nausea, excessive questioning of parents, and excessive fears (US Department of Health and Services 1999).

If symptoms of Separation Anxiety Disorder last longer than four weeks and cause significant distress in any areas of functioning, it is recommended that professional psychological or medical attention be sought immediately before it becomes a chronic problem. Treatment is more effective if it begins as soon as possible after the symptoms develop or begin manifesting themselves with any level of regularity or predictability.

Chapter 3

Trauma

Trauma is defined as a traumatic event that threatens injury, death, or the physical integrity of self or others and also causes horror, terror, or helplessness at the time it occurs. Traumatic events include sexual abuse, physical abuse, neglect, domestic violence, community and school violence, medical trauma, motor vehicle accidents, acts of terrorism, war experiences, natural and human made disasters, suicide, and other traumatic losses (Vassar 2011).

Trauma is not a unique experience for many children and adolescents. The following statistics from the Par Connections Report indicate that in community samples, more than two-thirds of children report experiencing a traumatic event by age sixteen. A child has a 39 to 85 percent estimated rate of witnessing community violence (Par Report 2013).

The estimated rate of victimization can be as high as 66 percent. A youth's exposure to sexual abuse is estimated to be between 25 and 43 percent. Children and adolescents make up a substantial proportion of the nearly 2.5 billion people affected worldwide by disasters in the past decade. It is more common than not for a child or adolescent to be exposed to more than one single traumatic event. Children exposed to chronic and pervasive trauma are especially vulnerable to the impact of subsequent trauma (Par Report 2013).

Children and adolescents respond differently to trauma, both behaviorally and emotionally. The short- and long-term impact of trauma depends on what the trauma is and where it happens as well as the race and ethnicity, poverty status, and gender of the child, which also affect the impact of trauma. Children exposed to chronic and pervasive trauma become vulnerable to the impact of subsequent trauma (APA 2015).

Symptoms may include the following: preschoolers: thumb sucking, bed-wetting, clinging to parents, sleep disturbances, loss of appetite, fear of the dark, regression in behavior, withdrawal from friends and routines;

elementary-school children: irritability, aggressiveness, clinginess, night-mares, school avoidance, poor concentration, withdrawal from activities and friends; adolescents: sleeping and eating disturbances, agitation, increases in conflicts, physical complaints, delinquent behavior, and poor concentration (Par Report 2013).

Youths who have been exposed to multiple traumas, have a past history of anxiety problems, or have experienced family adversity are likely to be at higher risk of showing symptoms of posttraumatic stress. It has been postulated that Post-Traumatic Stress Disorder may be in part the result of hyper-responsiveness of the amygdala.

All the new stress going on in the child's life seems to trigger a variety of responses that may be associated with PTSD (Eichenbaum and Cohen 2001). They explain in their findings and research that the over reactivity of the amygdala which is directly involved in attaching emotional valence to sensory information and the recurrent and intrusive traumatic memories as well as the excessive fear associated with traumatic reminders may be the hallmarks of PTSD.

The following is a list of assessments that may be useful in identifying possible trauma in children and adolescents:

Assessments of Trauma and Child Abuse:

1. Trauma Symptom Checklist for Young Children™ (TSCYC™).
2. Trauma Symptom Checklist for Children™ (TSCC™).
3. Trauma Symptom Checklist™ Software Portfolio (TSC™-SP).
4. Checklist for Child Abuse Evaluation (CCAE).
5. Child Sexual Behavior Inventory (CSBI™).
6. House-Tree-Person and Draw-A-Person as Measures of Abuse in Children: A Quantitative Scoring System (H-T-P/D-A-P).

Assessments of Depression:

7. Reynolds Child Depression Scale™, 2nd Ed. and Short Form (RCDS™-2 and RCDS™-2:SF).
8. Reynolds Adolescent Depression Scale, 2nd Ed. and Short Form (RADS-2™ and RADS-2™:SF).
9. Clinical Assessment of Depression™ and Scoring Program (CAD™ and CAD™ SP).
10. Adolescent Psychopathology Scale™ and Short Form (APS™ and APS-SF™).
11. Personality Assessment Inventory®-Adolescent (PAI®-A).
12. Reynolds Depression Screening Inventory™ (RDSI™).

Assessments of Anxiety/Irritability:

13. Adolescent Psychopathology Scale™ and Short Form (APS™ and APS-SF™).
14. Personality Assessment Inventory®-Adolescent (PAI®-A).
15. Clinical Assessment of Behavior™ (CAB™).

Assessments of Behavioral Disturbances (sleep disruption, acting out, loss of appetite, somatic complaints):

16. Emotional Disturbance Decision Tree™ (EDDT™).
17. Eyberg Child Behavior Inventory™ (ECBI™).
18. Sutter-Eyberg Student Behavior Inventory-Revised™ (SESBI-R™).
19. Clinical Assessment of Behavior™ (CAB™).
20. Pediatric Behavior Rating Scale™ (PBRS™).
21. Personality Assessment Inventory®-Adolescent (PAI®-A).
22. Revised Behavior Problem Checklist-PAR Edition (RBPC).
23. Children's Aggression Scale™ (CAS).
24. Reynolds Adolescent Adjustment Screening Inventory™ (RAASI™).

Assessments of Interpersonal Relationships:

25. Parenting Stress Index™, 4th Ed. (PSI™-4).
26. Stress Index for Parents of Adolescents™ (SIPA™).
27. Clinical Assessment of Interpersonal Relationships™ (CAIR™).

Risk Assessments:

28. Psychosocial Evaluation & Threat Risk Assessment™ (PETRA™).
29. Structured Assessment of Violence Risk in Youth™ (SAVRY™).
30. Suicidal Ideation Questionnaire (SIQ).
31. Adolescent & Child Urgent Threat Evaluation™ (ACUTE™).
32. Firestone Assessment of Violent Thoughts™-Adolescent (FAVT™-A).

(APA 2015; Par Connections Report 2013)

The above list of assessments is meant as beginning point for identification of PTSD and/or trauma issues. It is highly recommended that you work with a mental health professional or psychologists in the use of any of these psychological assessments.

CASE STUDY: JENNIFER, SIXTH GRADE

Jennifer was a transfer student to my classroom after Hurricane Katrina. She came into the class after being forced to come to the Northeast to stay with family. Their home had been completely destroyed. She was very shy, always looked very worried about something. Anytime there was a change of routine, new person in the class, or someone wanted to speak to her outside of class, she became extremely agitated and visibly shook.

Every time there were rain storms outside, you could see a visible change in her body movements, ability to pay attention, and her constant looking out the window. In talking with the parents they too had noticed that she was very nervous during any type of storm and would often have nightmares if there was thunder and excessive downpours.

Her fears and anxieties seem to depend on what was happening with the weather or whether a significant person in her life could be in danger. Because of this constant anxiety I asked the school counselor to work with Jennifer and I to relieve some of the tension and anxiety. The school counselor developed a check-in plan so that if there was a storm she could call her parents and see if everything was alright and if they were safe. Once she knew that everything was okay she could then concentrate on her schoolwork and begin interacting with her classmates (Lebrun 2007).

Additional Note: This example shows emotional memories triggering stress with a clearly identifiable source of the trauma. Once identified the plan can be made. Sometimes however there is no identifiable source for the trauma (often due to denial) and yet emotional memories are triggered and the stress response ensues. Teachers should be attuned to the odd behaviors and be aware that sometimes the trauma event(s) are too buried to be brought to consciousness. Yet, we still have to deal with posttraumatic stress (or trauma that may be occurring in the present).

RISK AND RESILIENCY FACTORS FOR PTSD

There are several risk factors that contribute to the acceleration and manifestation of PTSD. The key as educators is to figure out what is happening for the child or adolescent. The following risk factors should be noted:

a. Severity: it goes without saying that the more serious the trauma, the more likely it is to have long-lasting effects. For example, long-term abuse, will have a lifetime effect on many children.
b. Physical injury: a child who is physically injured in an event may feel trauma more intensely. For example, a child who has survived but been injured in a car accident or while skiing or swimming might then become fearful of that activity.
c. Involvement: those children directly involved in a traumatic event as opposed to just being a witness or bystander are more likely to

experience PTSD. The closer the proximity to the experience, the more likely the effects will be long lasting.

d. History: children who have experienced trauma in the past are more likely to be severely affected by another traumatic event. It seems that trauma builds upon itself and continues to add layers of dysfunction and fear with each subsequent experience.

e. Family: family instability or dysfunction can make children more susceptible to PTSD. Since children learn from what they are modeled, it becomes evident that they take on the same dysfunctional patterns as the adults in their lives, as there may not be any other more suitable models available to them.

(O'Brien and Ristuccia 2007)

RESILIENCY FACTORS

The two most important factors in helping children successfully manage PTSD are social and family supports and their coping mechanisms. It is a fact that positive support from family members and others who care for a student can help reduce an event's effect. Can a significant adult take away the stress of PTSD absolutely? Can they remove the memory? Probably not! What educators and parents can do is to provide multiple anxiety-reducing strategies that a child can tap into when they are feeling anxiety or stress.

There are two components to building resiliency: one is to teach the child how to recognize the triggers, contexts, and situations that lead to excessive stress and immediately seek assistance or use one of the anxiety-reducing techniques taught. The second is to increase their capacity to recognize the emotional and behavioral manifestations of stress themselves. For instance, when a child reacts to something angrily, they can be aware that the angry response is a manifestation of stress and this awareness could lead them to a more targeted solution.

CLASSROOM STRATEGIES AND INTERVENTIONS

Educators have varying expertise in dealing with trauma. Veteran teachers who have been in the classroom for years seem to manage some traumas more successfully because of the continued exposure over the years. Teachers who have dealt with students who have reported being physically or sexually abused are very aware of their responsibilities and the protocols and procedures they must follow as dictated by federal and state regulations.

In some cases, teachers are not aware of what the child has experienced because of confidentiality, or the parents are extremely secretive about the incident or situations. Sometimes the parent and/or child himself are not really aware of the traumatic event due to denial. This lack of openness may cause the educator to respond inappropriately, not because of lack of compassion or empathy, but out of ignorance.

The best antidote to secrecy is showing empathy and a genuine interest in the student and their lives. If an adult reaches out on a personal level it will build trust and the student is more likely to share some of the details of the trauma. Once you are informed of the trauma, it is imperative that you work with other support staff to provide any additional psychological or physical support as needed.

The following strategies, suggested by the (National Child Trauma Stress Network 2008) are generic in nature and are meant to begin the process of helping students cope with PTSD. They are not offered as a cure all or magic solutions, but as beginning points to lessen the impact of any emotional or physical reactions when a student is triggered.

1. Create a sense of safety and security in students. If students come to a classroom feeling that it is a safe place where they hear many positive words of comfort and encouragement the student will feel the teacher is approachable. Part of helping a student with PTSD is to work with the student to recognize their own feelings, triggers, and reactions, and to help them understand that they are not bad or crazy but feeling overwhelmed. Sometimes, if appropriate, helping the peers in the classroom become more encouraging with supportive behaviors or responses will support the student who has had the trauma (O'Brien and Ristuccia 2007).

2. Be especially sensitive to a student's background: students who live in urban settings and are exposed to gangs and community and school violence on a daily basis are more likely to have PTSD. Understanding the community, the school culture, and the climate in the building will all be instrumental in helping the students cope. Students who have emigrated from war-torn countries or have come from specific regions (Islamic, Southeast Asia, Africa) may be more at risk for PTSD. Do your research to figure out the conditions that these students have left and what they have experienced. Better understanding on your part will lead to better relationships with these students.

3. Provide a safe place when students become overwhelmed: So what happens when a student is triggered by a class discussion, a project, a story, or a conflict with a classmate and the memories and associations come flooding in. The best strategy is to have a designated space that is identified as safe, easily attainable, and has direct supervision. It is not acceptable to have the student removed forcibly, but to have this prearranged space

designated before any crisis occurs. The student is aware of the space, knows how to access the space, and is able to do so with little to no adult direction. The follow-up step is to inform a school counselor, administrator, or other significant individual who is aware of the student's difficulty and issue and will be supportive and not trigger additional stress.

4. Modify academic requirements: students often become overwhelmed by the amount of curriculum that is covered in a classroom daily. For many students, this is a potential trigger for an episode. It is important that educators base curriculum accommodations upon the severity of a student's PTSD. Knowledge of the issues, triggers, and the accompanying behaviors will help in measuring the student's capacity to handle the workload. Some possible accommodations might include a reduction in workload, flexible deadlines, and/or alternative assignments. Empathy and awareness are instrumental making adaptations so that the student can successfully manage within the classroom.

5. Create a calm, predictable environment: students spend anywhere from 6.5–8 hours a day in schools and classrooms. School needs to be a safe place for them, as many have experienced events outside of their control and may become anxious when variations occur in routines. Lack of predictability in this setting may be the trigger that leads to acting out behaviors. Clear expectations, consistency, and routines are the hallmarks to creating a classroom where a student with PTSD is more likely to be successful and less reactive. Changes in routines like field trips, schedule change, and special events can all be stressful; however, advanced communication is the solution.

6. Speak with the school counselor, parents, and outside professionals working with the student: communication between all of the adults who work and interact with the student is imperative for success. Some families may not share any outside resources that they are using because of shame, secrecy, or lack of trust in school personnel. The goal is to create supportive network for the child, so creating open lines of communication, implementing therapeutic supports, and monitoring medications if applicable are all part of a collaborative effort with the same goal.

7. If a child discloses trauma: stay calm and composed. Children take their emotional cues from adults, so keep a neutral reaction, actively listen intently, and validate feelings: "It's normal to feel _____. You have been through a very tough experience." *Always* believe the child. They might deny it later or change their story, but that's a common and natural reaction to trauma. Assure them they have done nothing wrong and were right in telling someone. Respect privacy (suggest going somewhere quiet and private to talk).

Let children know you believe them and care about them. Be supportive: "I am glad you told me about this." They might feel like you are going to be mad at them for telling. Help the child feel comfortable. Listen patiently, as it might take time.

When doing data collection of the incident choose your words carefully so as to not guide or influence the reports or statements. Choose words carefully: "That bruise looks painful. Do you want to tell me how you got it?" Be honest about your next course of action—this will build trust. The safety of the child is the priority. Protect them at all costs and make sure the burden of responsibility falls only on the abuser—not on the victim. If you think the child is likely to be further abused as a result of the disclosure, contact Child Protective Services immediately.

What not to do: don't react with shock, disgust, or anger. Be aware of facial and bodily expressions and tone of voice. Do not judge the child or the situation. Do not interrupt or interject personal opinion or experience into the conversation. *Don't* give advice. Never question whether they are telling the truth.

Don't imply it was their fault or that they should have done something differently. ("Why didn't you tell the police?" "Why were you walking across campus alone in the dark?" "If you had told someone sooner. . . .") Don't ask why questions—"Why did he hit you?" They often don't know why and will get confused. They might even think you are implying they are partially responsible (Ramamoorfhy and Myers-Walls n.d.).

Don't force the child to talk. Don't press them for details you don't need. Don't correct or laugh at terms the child is using. Don't introduce new terms. By doing so, you are interfering with their disclosure and potentially affecting evidence. Don't ask leading questions like "Did you get that bruise when someone hit you?"

Such questions might put information or assumptions in their head. DON'T LIE! If you are not sure of the answer, say "I am not sure of an appropriate answer to that question." Don't force child to show injuries but allow him to do so if he is willing. DON'T ignore the situation or minimize its impact. Acknowledge that it occurred: "I am so sorry you had such a (scary, awful, traumatic) experience" (Ramamoorfhy and Myers-Walls n.d.).

What to say: find out information: "Wow. This sounds like something we need to talk about further. Can you tell me what happened?" If they are comfortable, ask about missing information: "Who was home at the time?" "What happened after that?" Reflect back their feelings: "It sounds like _____ really ____(hurt, scared) you." When they are crying/refusing to talk: "I can't imagine what you are going through, but I am here to support you in whatever way feels best" (Heath 2013).

If you think the conversation is getting too upsetting: "I can see you are getting very upset. It's important that we talk about this, but would you like to take a break?" Be sure to tell them when information warrants you to make a report or talk with parents, etc. If you don't tell them, they might later feel betrayed!

Class discussions can be a very impactful technique but must be handled with care. The following guidelines by the National Association of School Psychologists, 2001 have been proven successful on many occasions: Guide discussion, but don't lead. Asking questions and stating observations is a good way to do this. Find out how much they know: questions such as "Is there anything you're worried about?"; "Is there anything you wish to talk about?"; or simply "Did you hear about such and such event?" are good openers. Let them know it's okay to be upset.

Keep the focus on the children's feelings and not yours or the details of what occurred. Be accepting of and empathetic about a variety of different reactions. Tell them the truth. Keep details to a minimum. Simplify terms and language. Stick to the facts. Don't exaggerate or speculate about the future. Dispel rumors. Be sensitive to developmental age and feelings.

If you think an answer is too complicated for them to understand, try to put it as simply as possible. Encourage them to talk about their feelings: "What were you feeling at the time?" "How do you feel now?" "It sounds like that was extremely upsetting." Be sensitive to children who might not want to participate.

Stop any teasing, bullying, or insensitivity immediately. Introduce the school counselor or psychologist and let children know they are the ones to talk to if they need extra support. You can ask kids' opinions if you don't have an answer. You might let them know you are sad, too, but don't dwell on negative feelings.

What not to do during class discussions: refrain from adding graphic or upsetting details. *Don't lie*—Be honest! If you are not sure of the answer, say "I am not sure of an appropriate answer to that question." *Don't* promise it won't happen again. *Don't* dwell on the subject.

How to direct the discussion on the event or trauma that has occurred: If they ask why it happened: "I don't know why this happened, but I am sorry that it did." If you don't know the answer: "You know, that's really a good question. I need to think about that and give you an answer this afternoon." If you think the conversation is getting too upsetting or the answer might be too hard to hear: "I can see you are getting very upset. It's important that we talk about this, but would you like to take a break?" "I think the answer to that might be too hard for you to hear right now."

If something similar reminds them of a tragedy: "This weather makes me think about Hurricane Sandy, but I know this is just a regular rainstorm and not a hurricane." Use open-ended questions: "Tell me about what happened?"

Classroom discussion and topics will be dependent on age and developmental level of the students that are in the classroom. Here is a list of their recommendations from the National Child Trauma Stress Network, 2008:

1. For younger kids: keep explanations and answers short, simple, and developmentally appropriate. Balance discussion with reassurances about safety and daily routines remaining the same.
2. For upper elementary/middle school: they will voice more concerns and want more detailed explanation or specifics about what is being done to ensure their safety. They will need support determining what is real and what is imagined.
3. For upper middle school/high school: they will be more vocal about opinions and what should be done to prevent future tragedies. They might want to get involved in helping efforts. Let all kids know they are safe (as long as they are!). Use specifics to support that claim.

In general, there are a variety of strategies that have proven to be effective when dealing with trauma at a school or in a classroom: For community tragedies especially, monitor the headlines and news regarding the trauma in order to be prepared for fallout in the classroom. Trials, sentencing, etc. might cause an increase in stress levels. Be careful not to portray stereotypes of countries/ethnicities involved in violence. Focus on tolerance and justice and not revenge.

Keep the focus on feelings and not graphic details. Choose words carefully. Terms such as "acts of war" can produce images or assumptions that might be incorrect. It can help children feel less helpless if they participate in the healing process. Consider group activities such as making thank you cards for emergency or aid workers or for the victims. Follow rules of confidentiality, mandated reporting, and referral. Make sure to inform parents (Buchler 2013).

PROFESSIONAL TREATMENTS

Professional treatment for anxiety usually involves some level of psychotherapy, medication, or alternative methods. Cognitive Behavioral Therapy (CBT) in many studies has been shown to be highly effective for PTSD (Birmaher et al. 1998; Heldt et al. 2003). Because every child reacts differently to traumatic events in his or her own way, it is important to listen and try to understand children's unique perspectives and concerns as well as those of the family.

CBT will often incorporate talk therapy, family therapy, and individual counseling for the child, and/or family together. When seeking out professional help, it is important to consider that families from ethnic or racial minority groups may encounter additional barriers, including limited access to services, insensitivity from the majority culture regarding the impact of racism and poverty, and finally language.

CBT has been shown to be very effective in treating children with PTSD. This treatment includes opportunities for the child or adolescent to review trauma in a safe, secure environment under the guidance of a specially trained mental health professional. CBT helps children with cognitive distortions related to the trauma. It can also provide direction and/or specific strategies on how to deal with, regulate, or control thoughts of self-blame, irrational, unrealistic, or negative thoughts. CBT will also guide the child to develop more adaptive understandings and perceptions of the trauma.

CBT has the most scientific evidence of efficacy in decreasing PTSD symptoms in traumatized children (Cohen at al. 2000). CBT is founded upon two specific core components: cognitive processing and exposure. These core components guided by the trained professional directly address the deficits in thinking or paradigms. The technique of cognitive processing teaches the child to examine and reframe the meaning of the trauma and any related experiences tied to the trauma.

It asks that the child look at their thoughts in a more evaluative way, thus asking the child to question and challenge the thoughts creating stress. Exposure techniques decondition the child's learned fear reactions to thoughts and discussions about the trauma. In other words the child is able to process and face the fears head on and address them with strategies that are directly taught.

Anxiety appears to be highly amenable to Selective Serotonin Reuptake Inhibitors (SSRIs) as a form of medication (Gotzsche 2014). A combination of both therapy and medication was found to be superior to both monotherapies (80.7 percent effective for combination therapy vs. 59.7 percent for just the CBT alone [Walkup et al. 2008]). Many of the medications presently used have been very effective with adults but there have been few to none tested for children. In many cases it becomes a guessing game that has many potential side-effects that outweigh the benefits of the medications.

Alternative therapies may include yoga, mindfulness training, nature explorations, guided imagery, exercise, using affirmations, sleep, meditation, and anything that can be used to relax oneself when in chaos or experiencing a stressful memory or flashback (Brown et al. 2006).

Helping Students Manage Emotions

In order to manage emotions, students need to be able to: recognize physical signs, be able to label how they are feeling, learn and use coping mechanisms to control arousal, and choose appropriate behavioral responses (O'Brien and Ristuccia 2007).

Helping students negotiate their world is also key as part of any type of intervention. We need to help students learn that their actions can make things happen. We do that by building social competence, confidence, and independence.

The practical application strategy is that we use Direct Instruction to teach social skills in the following sequence: pre-teach skills, connect them to previous learning using concrete examples; incorporate hands-on activities, role-playing, or games to engage students and make it fun; use scaffolding to guide student's choices and decision-making processes; practice skills as often as possible; create deliberate opportunities for successes; recognize and celebrate successes; and encourage independence (O'Brien and Ristuccia 2007).

Narrative Stories

Children tell the story of their experience and adults help those correct distortions in their rendition of what occurred or in their interpretation of the event. For example, children might think they were acting badly and so were hit because they deserved it. Adults need to let them know that it was not their fault and that it was wrong of the adult to hit them, that violence is never an answer, and hurting someone is always wrong.

Children might also get details mixed up: It rained so much that it flooded the neighborhood. This might cause heightened anxiety, as they become afraid when it rains. Setting them straight can reduce their anxiety: "The dams broke and caused the flood. They were old dams and now we have new ones built especially to handle hurricanes" (Buchler 2013).

Positive thinking techniques have also proven to be beneficial: Child identifies the negative self-talk that occurs to make him anxious. "I always fail at math." This can be difficult for young kids: using cartoons to illustrate their thoughts in different situations can help. For older children, journaling is a good way for them to discover how their thoughts affect their feelings.

Teach children to substitute these statements with positive or neutral ones. "I am still learning my multiplication tables. I just need more practice to learn them." Challenge their thinking: "What do you mean by 'fail'? You got a C on your report card. That means you must have had some successes in math." Teach them to challenge their own negative thoughts (Buchler 2013; Clay 2014).

Use positive approaches: disparaging comments, sarcasm, or punishment will only make them feel worse about themselves. It won't change behavior. Keep a positive attitude: "I know it feels overwhelming, but you can do this." Help them see the positive: "Hey, you finished over half of these by yourself!" (Clay 2014).

Focus on *progress*, not outcome: "You might have lost the game, but you made some great bounce passes and played wonderful defense" (Clay 2014).

Humor can work wonders. Teach students to use positive self-talk: "I can do it. It's important to try," or "It's okay to make mistakes" (Buchler 2013).

Strategies for improving self-regulation are always important to have in a tool kit for children. Treatment includes but is not limited to what professionals do, but what can be taught directly to the child on a daily basis in the safety of a classroom or school. Help kids learn to identify when they begin to get anxious. Make a fear scale with several levels of anxiety and draw or describe what each stages feels and looks like (Wagner 2005).

Use a signal system so the child can make the teacher aware of the anxiety level. Identify strategies they should use at each stage to self-calm: deep breathing, positive thinking, and relaxation. Make a plan for when anxiety becomes overwhelming—child goes to quiet area and reads or listens to music for a few minutes—child goes to school counselor.

Deep Breathing: breathing slowly and deeply, making the abdomen and chest expand completely and then exhaling slowly and completely. Room is quiet, eyes closed, and focus is on breath. There are multiple Apps for use in classroom found on the IPAD (Buchler 2013).

Progressive Relaxation: tensing and then relaxing various muscle groups, starting with the hands and progressing to the arms, shoulders, head, chest/back, abdomen, buttocks, legs, feet (Buchler 2013).

Imagery: closing eyes and imagining them in a happy, relaxing place. Picturing them successfully doing what causes them anxiety and practicing relaxation simultaneously (Buchler 2013).

Interventions, strategies, treatments are all part of the process toward the management of the symptoms of stress because at this time there has not been an identified cure. There isn't a cure because each individual processes stress and trauma differently. What we have been successful doing is teaching and building self-awareness, stress-management and coping skills for many individuals.

Unfortunately, as long as there are wars, natural disasters, inhumane treatment of people, abuse, violence, aggression, neglect, and cruelty, we will always have trauma in our midst. The best solution is to empower children to learn how to manage their thoughts and emotions in a way that allows them to be successful and interact with others in a healthy way. We can only do this by teaching and modeling what healthy thinking and actions are. The responsibility lies with the adults in the child's world.

Chapter 4

Mental Illness and Stress

Mental illness originates in the brain and influences all aspects of a child's life. Mental Illness can be manifested in psychological difficulties such as depression and anxiety. Hormonal or neurotransmitter chemical levels can impact emotional well being. What happens when these levels are disrupted or problematic? What happens when areas of the brain are affected in such a way that children feel depressed, anxious, or dangerously aggressive?

Presently about five million children in the United States have some type of mental illness that significantly interferes with daily life. Approximately 2 percent of children per year are diagnosed with a mental illness. This number is worrisome (Hasler 2011). What are the reasons or origins of mental illness? There are many theories, such as problems in areas of the brain or in brain development, insufficient or over stimulation of hormone or neurotransmitter levels in the brain, damaged DNA, toxins in the air and water, poor parenting, genetic predisposition, uncertainty and insecurity in our society, poor schools and communities.

THE FACTS (NAMI 2013)

1. 13% of youth aged 8–15 live with mental illness severe enough to cause significant impairment in their day-to-day lives. This figure jumps to 21% in youth aged 13–18.
2. Half of all lifetime cases of mental illness begin by age 14 and three-quarters by age 24. Early identification and intervention improve outcomes for children, before these conditions become far more serious, more costly and difficult to treat.

3. Despite the availability of effective treatment, there are average delays of eight to ten years between the onset of symptoms and intervention—critical developmental years in the life of a child. In our nation, only about 20% of youth with mental illness receive treatment.
4. Unidentified and untreated mental illness is associated with serious consequences for children, families, and communities. Approximately 50% of students aged 14 and older with mental illness drop out of high school—the highest dropout rate of any disability group.
5. Over 90% of those who die by suicide have a mental illness. Suicide is the third leading cause of death for youth aged 15–24; more youth and young adults die from suicide than from all natural causes combined.
6. Over 70% of youth in state and local juvenile justice systems have mental illness, with at least 20% experiencing severe symptoms. At the same time, juvenile facilities fail to adequately address the mental health needs of youth in their custody.
7. Untreated mental health problems can disrupt children's functioning at home, school and in the community. Without treatment, children with mental health issues are at increased risk of school failure, contact with the criminal justice system, dependence on social services, and even suicide.

(NAMI 2013)

Parents and family members are usually the first to notice if a child has problems with emotions or behavior. Observations, along with those of teachers and other caregivers, can help determine whether you need to seek help for the child.

Signs may indicate the need for professional help.

Symptoms in children vary depending on the type of mental illness, but here are some of the general symptoms identified by NAMI 2013:

1. Abuse of drugs and/or alcohol
2. Inability to cope with daily problems and activities
3. Changes in sleeping and/or eating habits
4. Excessive complaints of physical ailments
5. Defying authority, skipping school, stealing, or damaging property
6. Intense fear of gaining weight
7. Long-lasting negative moods, often accompanied by poor appetite and thoughts of death
8. Frequent outbursts of anger
9. Changes in school performance, such as getting poor grades despite good efforts
10. Loss of interest in friends and activities they usually enjoy

11. Significant increase in time spent alone
12. Excessive worrying or anxiety
13. Persistent nightmares or night terrors
14. Persistent disobedience or aggressive behavior
15. Frequent temper tantrums
16. Hearing voices or seeing things that are not there (hallucinations)
17. Decline in school performance
18. Poor grades despite strong efforts
19. Repeated refusal to go to school or to take part in normal activities
20. Hyperactivity or fidgeting
21. Depression, sadness, or irritability.

(National Institute of Mental Health 2013)

Because parents and teachers are on the front lines, interacting daily with children and adolescents, they are in an ideal position to detect potentially developing problems. Educators and parents need to be keen observers for any types of behavioral or cognitive changes that occur when a child is highly stressed or challenged or in situations that the response to a stimulus is much more extensive or radical than it should be for the child or for a child that age.

A variety of causes may be responsible for mental illness in children and adolescents: environmental factors such as fearful experiences, chronic stress or worry, or even a lack of oxygen in areas with high pollution or high elevation; physical/medical factors such as medical illness, medication side-effects, anemia, or asthma; substance abuse (particularly stimulants or withdrawal from depressants); genetic factors (family history); and brain chemistry (higher levels of certain neurotransmitters such as cortisol, hormones that stimulate the neuronal connections such as estrogen/testosterone) (NAMI 2013).

There are several different types of disorders that can affect children and adolescents, including:

1. Anxiety disorders: children with anxiety disorders respond to certain things or situations with fear and dread, as well as with physical signs of anxiety (nervousness), such as a rapid heartbeat and sweating.
2. Attention-deficit/hyperactivity disorder (ADHD): children with ADHD generally have problems paying attention or concentrating, can't seem to follow directions, and are easily bored and/or frustrated with tasks. They also tend to move constantly and are impulsive (do not think before they act).
3. Disruptive behavior disorders: children with these disorders tend to defy rules and often are disruptive in structured environments, such as school.

4. Pervasive development disorders: children with these disorders are confused in their thinking and generally have problems understanding the
world around them.
5. Eating disorders: eating disorders involve intense emotions and attitudes,
as well as unusual behaviors associated with weight and/or food.
6. Elimination disorders: disorders that affect behavior related to using the
bathroom. Enuresis, or bed-wetting, is the most common of the elimination disorders.
7. Learning and communication disorders: children with these disorders
have problems storing and processing information, as well as relating
their thoughts and ideas.
8. Affective (mood) disorders: these disorders involve persistent feelings of
sadness/depression and/or rapidly changing moods, and include depression and bipolar disorder.
9. Schizophrenia: this disorder involves distorted perceptions and thoughts.
10. Tic disorders: these disorders cause a person to perform repeated, sudden,
involuntary (not done on purpose), and often meaningless movements
and sounds, called tics.

(WEBMD 2014)

This is but a short list of what constitutes challenges for youth and children.
There is a continuum of mental health challenges that are being manifested
in our schools and communities. These disorders come in different degrees
of severity and are often seen over a continuum of difficulty. Some of these
disorders may co-exist with others and in so doing may confuse the adults or
the educators working with the student.

Co-morbidity is very common and therefore specific observations are
essential to ensure that the criteria for the disorder is clearly met and documented over a period of time. The Diagnostic Manual of Mental Health Disorders is an excellent reference for the specific criteria.

Best practices:

1. Give children unconditional love. Children need to know that your love
does not depend on their accomplishments.
2. Nurture children's confidence and self-esteem. Praise and encourage them.
Set realistic goals for them. Be honest about your mistakes. Avoid sarcasm.
3. Encourage children to play. Play time is as important to a child's development as food. Play helps children be creative, develop problem-solving
skills and self-control, and learn how to get along with others.
4. Treatment consists of enrolling children in an after school activity, especially if they are otherwise home alone after school. This is a great way for
kids to stay productive, learn something new, gain self-esteem, and have

something to look forward to during the week. Check in on children after school if they are home alone. Children need to know that even if you're not there physically, you're thinking about them, and interested in how they spent their day and how they'll spend the rest of it.

5. Provide a safe and secure environment. Fear can be very real for a child. Try to find out what is frightening him or her. Be loving and patient and reassuring, not critical.

6. Give appropriate guidance and discipline when necessary. Be firm, but kind and realistic with your expectations. The goal is not to control the child, but to help him or her learn self-control.

7. Communicate. Make time each day after work and school to listen to your children and talk with them about what is happening in their lives. Share emotions and feelings with your children.

8. Get help. If you're concerned about your child's mental health, consult with teachers, a guidance counselor or another adult who may have information about his or her behavior. If you think there is a problem, seek professional help. Early identification and treatment can help children with mental health problems reach their full potential.

(Mental Health America 2000)

We need to understand whether current treatments can be used with children and families who experience a variety of diverse traumas, stressful contexts, or the early onset of mental illness. Because there is so much variability in levels of stress and traumas, a cookie cutter approach must be abandoned and replaced with a much more clearly identified adaptable approach. There has to be more in-depth research undertaken to test the specific efficacy of several techniques for stress management.

We also need to develop better access and delivery for families who have mentally ill children. Professionals in the mental health arena need to have practical, flexible and feasible tools that they can incorporate or use to augment what they presently have at their disposal. We need to have these tools and resources ready when families reach out for help.

Medication is the most common treatment for children with mental illness. Medication targets areas of the brain acted upon by for the hormones or neurotransmitters responsible for the problems. For example a class of drugs used to treat major depression is the Selective Serotonin Reuptake Inhibitors (SSRI) which works by affecting the reabsorption of serotonin in the brain. This affects the balance of serotonin in the brain and leads to mood improvement.

These classes of drugs are sometimes also used to treat anxiety. ADHD medication works to restore the balance of stimulant neurotransmitters in the brain (dopamine and norepinephrine), they are important for memory formation, arousal, and attention. In addition, researchers have also shown that ADHD drugs target areas responsible for attention, impulse control, and decision-making in the frontal lobe of the brain.

One of the important factors impacting families with mentally ill children is the stress that can result from increase in managed care restrictions. Such restrictions have resulted in fewer health treatment sessions being approved as well as higher copayments. Many families cannot afford proper treatments. Finally, there is a lack of therapists on approved provider panels with the appropriate expertise in treating mentally ill children.

Health care companies have been very clear in their mandate that they will support children seeing a physician rather than a therapist, and that has resulted in much more emphasis on pharmacology rather than psychotherapy. This is disturbing in that nonpsychiatrists are prescribing psychotropic medications to children and adolescents. A change in the way business is done is needed to meet the needs of mentally ill children. There will need to be an increase in insurance coverage for mental health treatment and more funding for training and oversight for general physicians who work with children and adolescents.

The role of mental health professionals needs to expand beyond clinics or doctors' offices. Mental health consultations must occur in an outreach mode in which they are present to deliver onsite and integrated services in health care, school, spiritual, social justice and other service systems settings. The availability and access is crucial to encouraging families to reach out in a time of need. These professionals can become advocates for the families.

Without treatment, many mental disorders can continue into adulthood and lead to problems in all areas of the person's adult life. People with untreated mental disorders are at high risk for many problems, including alcohol or drug abuse, and (depending on the type of disorder) violent or self-destructive behavior, even suicide.

When treated appropriately and early, many children can fully recover from their mental disorder or successfully control their symptoms. Although some children become disabled adults because of a chronic or severe disorder, many people who experience a mental illness are able to live full and productive lives.

The role of stress in challenging our ability to handle day-to-day circumstances is paramount to our ability to handle difficult traumas, experiences, or mental health challenges. Stress is a manifestation of our lives and our times. There is a definite need to teach the next generations the skills in being able to be aware of their own stress, to recognize when it is happening, and to have tools to manage it effectively to achieve better outcomes in their daily lives.

Chapter 5

Anger and Stress

The Dynamic Duo!

Anger is an acid that can do more harm to the vessel in which it is stored than to anything on which it is poured.

Mark Twain

We all get angry; it's a normal emotion. However, some of us handle our anger better than others. Anger is an individual response. How can the same event cause such different reactions? How can an adult help a child or adolescent make sure that the reaction is the calm one, instead of the impulsive one? Subjectivity can make anger difficult to understand and manage. It also highlights that the response to anger is entirely within the control of the individual person.

According to psychologist T. W. Smith, anger is "an unpleasant emotion ranging in intensity from irritation or annoyance to fury or rage" (Mindtools. com). Every day, we experience things that could make us angry. Frequent causes of anger include frustration, hurt, harassment and injustice, regardless of whether real or perceived; requests or criticisms that we believe are unfair; and threats to people, things, or ideas that we hold dear. People experience anger in different ways and for different reasons. The challenge lies in providing a variety of strategies for intervention.

Educators need to understand how stress and anger feed off one another. We have children who are so stressed out by daily routines in a classroom that they become completely overwhelmed; thus, their only response is to act out to release the stress. These are two crucial events! One is definitely the adult's reading of and reaction to the child's stress response. The other is preventing stress responses through knowledge of the students and using good education practices, such as teaching children to recognize their triggers, responses, and effective stress reduction strategies. It is important in helping children to realize that the immediate relief that is gained by some of the acting out (or avoidance) behaviors, may result in long-term costs. This is the same for adults; the initial anger caused by the stress of a disruptive student causes the adult to act impulsively to get immediate relief but actually costs them in the long term.

The actions and reactions of the adults to the manifestation of this behavior either creates an environment which fosters anger and aggression or calms the child and dissipates the stress. The adult's response often has the power to either deescalate or increase anger. Unfortunately, adults sometimes (often depending on their own stress level and training), do not consider the impact of their own actions and words, and will blame the student for noncompliance, defiance or disrespect. The result is often escalating emotion and behavior (for both adult and student).

Anger is not always an incorrect response. Anger can motivate individuals to become advocates for change, stand up for injustices, or problemsolve in a more creative or analytical way. The behavioral manifestation of the anger is the key to success or dysfunction in the school environment. If anger is used as a coping mechanism it often will result in relationships that are insecure, marked with emotional highs and lows, and result in strained relationships between adults and children.

Anger manifested frequently in both adults and children has led to health risk (Staicu and Cutov 2010). The literature demonstrates that anger, whether suppressed or expressed, can increase various diseases, aggravate the symptoms of bulimia nervosa, or cause car accidents. The research indicated direct correlations between anger and coronary heart disease, diabetes, and several other related physical and emotional diseases.

Since stress increases anger, it is common sense that both educators and children need to be taught how to recognize stress and its triggers, as well as solutions for management of the stress before it becomes anger. Educators struggle with students who have Opposite Defiant Disorder and Conduct Disorder in the classroom on a daily basis. The following are characteristics that often accompany ODD:

Behavioral Definitions as defined in *APA Diagnostic Manual of Mental Disorders* (fifth edition):

1. Pattern of negativistic, hostile, and defiant behavior toward all adults.
2. Acting as if parents, teachers, and other authority figures are the enemy.
3. Temper tantrums (e.g., screaming, crying, throwing objects, thrashing on the ground, or refusing to move) in defiance of direction from an adult caregiver.
4. Constant arguing with adults.
5. Defying or refusing to comply with requests and rules even they are reasonable.

6. Deliberate annoyance of people and susceptibility to annoyance from others.
7. Blaming others for his/her mistakes or misbehavior.
8. Consistent display of anger and resentment.
9. Frequent display of spite and vindictiveness.
10. Significant impairment in social, academic, or occupational functioning due to obstreperous behaviors.

These behaviors are easily identified, but it is important for educators to document and recognize patterns of anger. The purpose of identifying patterns of anger through the collection of data is to be able to plan effective interventions and supports based on reliable behavior patterns. Observers in the classroom must be able to document the frequency, intensity, time, and length of the episodes before being able to plan any type of effective interventions. A predictable pattern of behavior has to be observed and documented over time to show a consistent pattern or reliability of the behavior sequence (triggers, antecedents, behaviors, and consequences).

The goals of any intervention plan must focus on the following objectives:

1. Reduce the frequency and intensity of the behaviors.
2. Terminate temper tantrums and replace with calm, respectful compliance with adult directions.
3. Consistently interact with others in a mutually respectful manner.
4. Increase level of cooperation, respect, communication.
5. Give the student the opportunity to understand and become much more aware of how to resolve the conflict that underlies the anger, stress, hostility, and defiance.

(Jongsma et al. 1996)

Interventions for these types of students must be taught such that the student recognizes the cost and benefits of changing their behavior. It is unlikely that this type of student is ever going to change their behavior if the benefits of exhibiting this behavior allow them to receive reinforcement, rewards, or recognition. The adults must be cognizant of what they are reinforcing and how their strategies are getting the desired results. Below is a list of possible strategies/interventions that can be used directly in the classroom or in one on one sessions taught by a school counselor.

1. Build level of trust through consistent eye contact, active listening, unconditional positive regard, and warm acceptance to help increase his/her ability to identify and express feelings.
2. Encourage the student to verbalize the sources of negative, hostile feelings in an open, accepting, and understanding manner.

3. Process negative behaviors and offer a paradoxical interpretation or reframing of the behaviors.
4. Assist the student in becoming able to recognize feelings and express them in a respectful way. This may include the teaching of direct social skills.
5. Collaborate with the family to use clear guidelines and expectations in terms of behaviors in school and at home.
6. Work in collaboration with the parents to implement a behavior modification contract that is enforced and created in conjunction with the teachers, students, and administrators who deal with the student on a daily basis.

(Jongsma et al. 1996)

Dealing effectively with this type of student requires educators to be consistent and predicable, and to have clear and enforceable guidelines with reasonable, relevant, and respectful consequences. The adults become part of the solution but must also be very aware of their own contributions to the formation and exhibition of the student's defiant behaviors.

Working effectively with students with Conduct Disorder requires a clear understanding of the progression and increase of violent and aggressive behaviors that have now manifested out of Oppositional Defiance to the more severe Conduct Disorder label. Students who are identified as conduct disordered have reached a whole new level of intensity when it comes to acting out, brought on by stress, family, or contextual factors present in the student's life.

Conduct disordered students can often be identified with the following behavioral definitions from the *APA Statistical Manual of Disorders* (fifth edition):

1. Persistent failure to comply with rules or expectations in the home, school, and community.
2. Excessive fighting, intimidation of others, cruelty or violence toward people or animals, and destruction of property.
3. History of breaking and entering or stealing.
4. School adjustment characterized by repeated truancy, disrespectful attitude, and suspensions for misbehavior.
5. Repeated conflict or confrontations with authority figures at home, school, and community.
6. Failure to consider the consequences of actions, taking unnecessary risks, and engaging in thrill seeking behaviors.
7. Numerous attempts to deceive others through lying, conning, or manipulating.
8. Consistent failure to accept responsibility for misbehavior, accompanied by a pattern of blaming others.

9. Little or no remorse for past misbehavior.
10. Lack of sensitivity to the thoughts, feelings, and needs of other people.
11. Multiple sexual partners, lack of emotional commitment, and engaging in sexual relations that increase the risk for contracting sexually transmitted diseases.

As this list is quite extensive it is important to address that not all conduct disordered students manifest these behaviors at a level of extreme aggression or violence or criminality. Each individual is on a continuum of development and manifestation of these behaviors based on their life experiences and the amount of stress that is fueling their unacceptable behaviors. This group has the largest potential to move on to criminal behavior and future imprisonment.

When intervening with this population in a school setting, it is best to develop the following goals and/or objectives while teaching new coping mechanisms or positive cognitive thinking patterns:

1. Demonstrate increased honesty, compliance with rules, sensitivity to the feelings and rights of others, control over impulses and acceptance of responsibility for his/her behavior.
2. Comply with rules and expectations in the home, school, and community on a consistent basis.
3. Eliminate all illegal and antisocial behaviors.
4. Terminate all acts of violence or cruelty toward people or animals and the destruction of property.
5. Express anger through appropriate verbalizations and healthy physical outlets on a consistent basis.
6. Demonstrate marked improvement in impulse control.
7. Resolve the core conflicts which contribute to the emergence of conduct problems.
8. Work with the parents to establish and maintain appropriate parent-child boundaries, setting firm, consistent limits when the student acts out in an aggressive or rebellious manner.
9. Demonstrate empathy, concern, and sensitivity for the thoughts, feelings, and needs of others on a regular basis.
10. Eliminate all sexually promiscuous behaviors.

(Jongsma et al. 1996)

Schools and educators can be at the forefront in helping this type of student master skills that are proactive and can help in stressful situations. Stress for these children will always increase potential for regression to old behaviors even after they've made progress. The process of retraining and re-teaching these students to become more aware of how their actions influence or impact others may be lifelong because of how deep the behaviors have become entrenched in the repertoire of skills the student possesses. The path to new behaviors has to be clearly articulated and implemented with a consistency that teaches, reinforces, and holds the student accountable for their actions. Building responsibility and accountability are the foundation of any type of change or intervention with this group of students.

The following interventions have proven to be successful when integrated into a behavior support plan:

1. Psychological psycho-educational testing and substance abuse and medical evaluations are often needed to get a baseline of student's functioning.
2. Work with the parents to establish clear guidelines, expectations, rules, boundaries, and consequences.
3. The use of restitution, community service, probation, and intense supervision has proven to be effective in changing behaviors.
4. Address the antisocial behaviors and attitudes by using cognitive restructuring techniques and strategies.
5. Assist the student to make connections between feelings, stress, and reactive behaviors.
6. Explore and process factors that contribute to blaming others and avoiding accepting responsibility.
7. Teach mediational and self-control strategies.
8. Teach effective communication and assertiveness skills to express feelings in a controlled fashion and meet their needs through constructive actions.
9. Design a reward system or contingency contracts to reinforce identified positive behaviors and deter impulsive behaviors.
10. Teach how to show empathy, kindness, or sensitivity to others.

(Jongsma et al. 1996)

The biggest factor for effective intervention with this population is the ability for them to become more aware of their triggers, their overreactions, and the self-defeating results of their overreactions. The second component is for these students to be able to self-monitor self-control and make better choices in the way they respond to stress in particular situations or with certain individuals.

The earlier the intervention and social skills training the more likely the student will be able to integrate these skills in their everyday reactions. It is key to building self-awareness and the belief that they have the power to change the outcomes of interactions based on what they do differently.

When working with students to help them understand how stress fuels their anger and the responses, therapy should focus on recognizing and challenging how their distorted thinking contributes to and directs the actions that at times may be self-destructive, violent, or aggressive toward others.

There are four major categories of cognitive distortions—Victim Mindset, Polarity Mindset, Emotional Mindset, and Perfectionist Mindset—and fifteen actual cognitive distortions (Beck 1979). Each of these categories influences the thinking, feelings, and actions of students and the adults who work with them. Each distortion is more likely to be triggered or be exacerbated by stress.

The Victim Mindset is based in feelings of inadequacy and low self-esteem. They might be targeted by others, feel unable to make decisions or take action, or believe that all of their responses are a result of others' actions and reactions. They do not see themselves as having a voice or strength to be creators of their own destiny; everything depends on others. This mindset creates a sense of hopelessness and helplessness that leads to insurmountable amounts of stress and inaction or overreaction to the stimuli that is presented in that particular context.

These students may manifest a variety of avoidance behaviors to escape from the situation in order to avoid responsibility for their actions and reactions. The solution to this mindset is to teach the student that they can have a say in the solutions and decisions that affect them. Their involvement is welcome and necessary to build ownership (Grohol 2015).

The Polarity Mindset is also an extreme response to stress. In polarized thinking, things are either "black or white." The student has to be perfect or he or she is a failure—there is no middle ground. Students or teachers place people or situations in "either/or" categories, with no shades of gray or allowing for the varied complexity of most people and situations. If a student's performance falls short of perfect, they see themselves as a total failure. The solution to this type of mindset is teaching the student to make informed decisions based on all the facts and not on perception (Grohol 2015).

The Emotional Mindset is composed of a series of cognitive distortions (Grohol 2015). This list includes filtering, overgeneralizations, jumping to conclusions, fallacy, fairness, shoulds, and personalization. The lens through which students interpret events is based on experiences, coping skills, and modeling observed in their interactions with the adults in their lives. The reactions will be healthy or dysfunctional based on those coping mechanisms available to them at the time of the stress. The solution to this source of stress is learning effective coping and problem-solving skills.

The Perfectionist Mindset is one that is instilled early on in life. It happens during the formative years of personality development. Children learn very quickly whether making mistakes is encouraged or discouraged. Parents' responses to the child's experimenting with new learning will dictate how the child perceives themselves and later defines their self-esteem.

"Practice ensures growth and development" needs to be at the forefront of the student's thinking as compared to "practice makes perfect," which is a cognitive shift that needs to happen so the student sees that effort, not final results, define the student and their actions.

Students in the school system want to receive "A" grades but often do not have the skills to achieve these grades. They are driven to the point of such anxiety and stress that they become physically and mentally ill trying to achieve unrealistic goals or expectations set by the adults in their lives. The solution is that perfection is never achieved; the journey of discovery is where the real learning happens.

In conclusion, the secret of success when dealing with students whose unmanaged or poorly managed stress tends to manifest in anger and who are struggling is to guide them a level of self-awareness of the triggers, the understanding of the cognitive distortions that are fueling the responses, and the ability to change their thinking by very specific strategies or coping skills.

As every athlete knows, you take a muscle, train it, challenge it repeatedly, use it frequently in the context that you have trained, and perform when asked or challenged. The same goes with students and how they effectively respond to stress and anger. We need to train the mind, so that the thoughts regulate the emotions to decrease stress and anger, and increase the likelihood of positive proactive responses and actions.

Chapter 6

Strategies and Interventions for Successful Stress Management

Our bodies weep the tears our eyes refuse to shed.

Sir William Osler

Stress reduction is a multibillion-dollar industry. The resources invested in trying to manage stress involves education, healthcare, business, and government. Stress is not a new concept but one that evolves as the human race evolves. New technologies, ideologies, and inventions all create a new way of doing something aimed at enhancing quality of life and above all producing a change.

Change is stressful, regardless of resulting benefits. Change is perceived differently because of one's own lenses and biases. An individual's adaptability to change is an area that needs to have a root cause analysis in order to achieve an acceptable level of equilibrium in one's life. The framework of change is built around the concepts of anticipating and welcoming change. Although many people accept that change is unavoidable, they still view it negatively. One must understand the source of the fear regarding change before any intervention strategies can be implemented effectively.

It is a known fact that people and organizations that understand and welcome change as an opportunity and know how to work with the changes are more likely to be successful. Peter Drucker said, "You can't manage change. You can only be ahead of it. You can only meet it." This mindset needs to be prevalent if institutions like schools and governments are to be proactive in preparing for change which is inevitable in our constantly evolving society.

Educators who are in a position of leadership need to understand that change is stressful. Stress is manifested from both a social context and a personal perspective. Students and teachers become stressed out because the changes are not well planned out, articulated or presented in a way that the receiver of the change is able to understand the expectations and act accordingly. Managing complex change is both an art and a science.

To achieve lasting change the leaders must possess the ability to identify a vision and the necessary skills to make the change happen, give incentives that are desirable for the audience needing to enact the change, ensure that resources are plentiful and supported over a designated period of time, and provide an action plan that is solidly based on clear and achievable goals and objectives. Change and education are synonymous with transition.

The transitions in education are daily: going from bus to classroom; going from whole group activity to individual work; new instructional topics; new activities; changing of grades; and going from middle to high school are all major and minor changes that are part of the daily life of a student and educator. Since transition is such a major part of school life and since it is a stress producer, the relevance of addressing transitions thoughtfully to reduce stress for students and educators is high.

For stress management to occur at the grassroots level in the schools and classrooms, effective change leaders must be able and willing to institute policies to make the present create the future. There should be ongoing discussions designed to evaluate current practices and phase out those that are no longer effective or meeting the needs of students and teachers. These discussions should include ideas for creative new solutions to replace these outdated practices, such as replacing overhead projectors with interactive smart boards.

Educational leaders need to provide systematic methods to look for and anticipate change in school and classroom organizational structures. Organized improvement is slow, systematic, involves the stakeholders in the discussions, and clearly outlines the steps and timeline to achieve the changes in a productive way.

Educational change leaders need to know the right ways to introduce change inside and outside of their schools, districts, or organizations and be able to exploit opportunities as they arise. Unfortunately, many school leaders have been handcuffed by standardization, budget restraints, and fiscal accountability that have prevented them from being forerunners in developing and advocating for change.

This lack of opportunity for innovation and creativity has funneled itself down to the schools and classrooms, where both staff and students are receiving the brunt of the restrictions or limitations imposed by those in power. It is a fine dance of being able to balance change and continuity. Leaders and teachers try to preserve trust and openness in such a way that it creates less stress. Having calmer educators will mean less stress being channeled down into the classrooms to the students.

CLASSROOM INTERVENTIONS AND STRATEGIES

Students and children who experience poor stress management and the accompanying behaviors often have a weakness in something called emotional intelligence (EQ), which indicates a lack of emotional regulatory skills. Daniel Goleman popularized the concept of EQ by defining it as a process that allows human beings to understand, regulate, and manage our emotions as key determinants of life successes and happiness.

Jeffrey Bernstein in his research "Liking the Child you Love" indicated that emotional intelligence appears to be a key predictor of children's ability to make suitable peer relationships, get along at home, and develop a well-balanced outlook on life and to reach their academic potential at school (Bernstein 2013).

Building EQ is a process that is very skill based and needs to be taught, not during a crisis or a period of intervention after conflict, but as a proactive preparation to enhance the student's ability to have these skills available to them in times of difficult situations or interactions. The following five characteristics and abilities are at the cornerstone of teaching EQ in children and adolescents:

Self-awareness: it is very difficult for many adults to understand and know their emotions and even more challenging for children and adolescents. Helping students to recognize their feelings as they occur, knowing the difference in each feeling, and the appropriate reaction is key to building this internal gauge which is self-awareness. Capacity for self-awareness like all stress skills is compromised during stress.

Therefore, the ability to observe oneself in the moment when the self-observation can actually prevent exacerbating problems is a compounded issue. This fact should be taught. When a student is stressed, he or she is less likely to be able to observe their perceptions, thoughts, and feelings accurately and thus select strategies that are best for them. Therefore the student is always better off implementing a strategy to reduce their stress before selecting a response strategy. The likelihood for an impulsive and costly action is increased when the student hasn't managed their stress.

Using posters for students to point out their feelings (angry, stressed, unhappy, happy, etc.) and attaching vocabulary that helps them articulate what is happening inside their bodies allows them to appropriately express, rather than repress these emotions.

Helping students to recognize what stress feels like physically and emotionally is key. One can do this by asking questions such as: how does your body feel when you are stressed? Are your muscles or stomach tight or sore? Are your hands clenched? Is your breath shallow? Questioning can occur till a child is able to see the physical impact of the stress.

Mood management is more of a challenge because this may not always be something that a student can control. Anxiety, depression, and responses to medication may play a role in the manifestation of additional or magnified stress responses. Teaching should be handled in a way that it is relevant to the current situation or conflict in such a way that the individual student and the adult have a reaction that is in line with the intensity or frequency of the conflict or the stress.

Everyone reacts to stress differently and therefore to stress relief activities that help them cope with the stress. For example, if a student is more depressed or withdrawn, stress relief activities (exercise) that are more stimulating might be more beneficial. If a student is more agitated or anxious or freezes up, stress relief activities (meditation, social interaction) that may speedup in some ways and slowdown in others might be beneficial in that they provide attention, comfort and stimulation.

Self-motivation is as varied as the individual person. Many students struggle to be motivated because of life experiences and have become unable to self-motivate because of the impact of stress. Students need to understand their feelings and figure out a way to direct themselves toward a goal and/or action that helps resolve the situation, despite self-doubt, inertia, and impulsiveness.

The individual student becomes motivated to make a change that will have a larger impact than just the immediate gratification of reacting to the issue at hand. Often, students react in ways that don't resolve the issue but aggravate the situation further. The student is able to be part of a change plan that is articulated with specific action steps toward achieving improvement of their life situation or decreasing the influence of the stress. Helping students engage their senses (sight, sound, smell, taste, and touch) to building stress relief may also be helpful.

Different sensory input produces different responses that may be more soothing or energizing for the student. For example a water fountain, scented candle, or music may all do the trick. Sustaining a change plan requires concurrent stress reduction-prevention and effective reduction. Stress will increase the need for immediate relief and will often sabotage progress toward long-term outcomes.

Stress management is therefore a balance of ensuring environmental stress reduction, teacher calmness and thoughtful-validating responses, as well as the student role in improving his/her capacity for self-awareness, implementation of effective strategies, and sustaining motivation to manage short-term stress in the interest of attaining longer-term goals.

Empathy is one of those human qualities that is thought to be a necessary requirement of being a good citizen or person. Empathy is often thrown into the mix of many interpersonal relationship dynamics without clearly teaching what it is. In the early years children develop it by seeing it happening through role-plays, discussions, and actual teaching during class time.

Recognizing the feelings of others and tuning into their verbal and nonverbal cues is extremely difficult for many people to do with a certain level of success and predictability. As children develop, we need to be continually directing the student to becoming more aware of how others are responding, reacting, or engaging with them. How do you think the other person feels? Would you like this to happen? If not let's look at why. Teaching by using stories or narratives that require the child to put himself in the shoes of others may help them to become more empathic over the years as they experience a variety of situations, people, and feelings.

One of the most profound impacts of stress is the compromised ability to see the perspective of others especially "in the moment." So empathy that is taught without concurrent teaching of stress awareness and stress management will be inherently less effective since empathy is far more difficult to access during stress events.

Managing relationships and the accompanying dynamics are a challenge, regardless of the amount of experience or maturity an individual has. The handling of daily interpersonal interactions is in constant flux, depending on who is in the student's life. Managing these interactions requires self-awareness and awareness of others and what they bring to the relationship, and how conflict and stress puts added pressures on relationships.

Teaching stress management involves actual teaching of conflict resolution, negotiation, and achieving successful resolution to issues. This is the ideal; the reality is that many students are not able to achieve the skills because of the level of emotional intensity that is attached to the situation or directed at the individual within the relationship. Helping students get to a place of resolution can only occur if the adults model excellent problemsolving and communication skills as they work with the student to rebuild the relationships within the context of the stressful situation.

The following Stress Busters are a quick reminder that sometimes addressing stress can mean a small change in behavior. It begins with scaffolding the change in attitude or actual behavior. The following Stress Busters can be taught easily to children and adolescents:

1. Reduce clutter: keep your things in order. Keeping clutter down reduces stress. The same applies to relationships, activities, and responsibilities. Keep things simple.
2. Do not be a control freak: let other people do whatever they want to do. With students it is important to offer choices and inform students on how to make an informed choice.
3. Do not let things and people get to you: remember that you cannot control many things that happen or how others behave. Try to take things as they come and do not allow yourself to get stressed out over them.

4. Look after you: a good diet, exercise, and plenty of sleep make a more well-balanced person capable of coping better with stressors.
5. Think positively: do not allow negative thinking take over your mind. Force yourself to think positively about situations you must face; it makes it easier to deal with them.
6. Live in the here and now: do not obsess about things that have already happened or things that may or may not occur in the future. It is best to live in today and effectively cope with today's events today.
7. Maintain a sense of humor: looking at stressors with a sense of humor can lessen the load for you and allow you to see them in a different light.
8. Be a winner, not a loser: be a helper to others—do not be a victim. By helping others, your own problems will be put into the proper perspective and will diminish in importance.
9. When feeling stressed, inhale deeply through your nose, hold, and slowly exhale through your mouth. Repeat 5–10 times. Oxygen relaxes the body. Develop the art of cruising in neutral. Develop the art of letting go. Get in touch with your moods.
10. Take a daily music break: with eyes closed, sit back and listen to ten minutes of soothing sound.
11. Give in when you have little to gain: save your energy for the important things.
12. When you're uptight and tense, relax muscle groups: start with the top of your head and work your way to your toes.

(Gordon 2015)

STEP BY STEP GUIDE TO BUILDING COPING STRATEGIES FOR STUDENTS

Teachers have an opportunity to teach students better coping strategies for stress management. This step by step guide can be done with an entire class, small groups, or individual students who are struggling with the stress in a variety of settings or with a variety of triggers. The process can be similar for many students but the plan that is created is unique to the individual or group.

Step 1: Summarize the Symptoms. Student is asked to summarize all the discomforts that are occurring during the day or during stressful times.
Step 2: Define the Problem Clearly. In discussion with the student, try to do a root cause analysis: where, when, why, what, and who are involved in the stressful activity or context.
Step 3: Identify the Resources. What kinds of strengths does the student have physically, socially, intellectually, and spiritually? Does the student have significant adult resources or mentors?

Step 4: Previous Interventions. Brainstorm with the student what has already been tried whether successfully or unsuccessfully and sort out the strategies that are more likely to be successful.

Step 5: Check the Attitude. The student's attitude toward the problem determines at least 50% of the end result. It is imperative that the student have a positive and healthy attitude or the potential to develop one if it is not presently obvious. Assure there is some synergy toward finding a solution. Assure that both adult and student see the need for some change.

Step 6: Define the Goals Clearly. What does the student want to happen? Develop goals that are doable and realistic. Make sure the goals are in line with the student's core values and beliefs.

Step 7: Formulate a Specific Plan of Action. Brainstorm and choose specific activities that will produce positive lasting rewards. Build a timetable for achievement of the goals and actions within the plan.

Step 8: Spice the Plan with Creativity. Make the activities fun and engaging. This will enrich and energize the experience for the student.

Step 9: Act—Do It. Get the student to actively engage by doing the plan. Reinforce and recognize the efforts as the student is making the changes.

Step 10: Evaluate the Results and Revise the Plan. No plan is forever. Test out the ideas, observe the effects, continue the actions that are working, drop the ones that are not working, and understand why they did not work. Reevaluate constantly as the behaviors and stress responses are being shaped. Whenever you have stress or new stress, go back and start the process again.

THREE SIMPLE MOVEMENTS TO STRESS MANAGEMENT

It is paramount in any type of stress management that students are taught how to recognize what is happening to them physically and awareness of their own stress triggers. Becoming more aware of the physical manifestations of stress allows the students to be self-aware of the triggers and hopefully deal with them more efficiently or quickly. This level of self-awareness becomes one of the best first responses to stressful situations.

The three stress simple movements are:

1. Step Back: this is where you teach the student to ask a series of questions to challenge the thoughts that may be creating the physical responses. There are several opportunities for self-awareness, awareness of physical manifestations, emotional manifestations, cognitive manifestations (negative thinking) and knowing stress triggers.

   The strategies listed below will be especially useful if a student can acknowledge the counterproductive outcomes of their own negative thinking. The following questions may help the student to step back: Is this going to matter in a day? Week? Month? Year? In the big picture of my life, how much does this really matter? Is there anyone who can help me with this? What is the worst thing that can happen? Have I done the best that I could under the circumstances? What are my expectations and fears?

2. Take a Deep Breath: stopping and breathing may be a simple thing to do but many students forget to breathe long and deep and begin breathing short and shallow. Students need to eat right, exercise regularly, sleep well, do some progressive relaxation, and tap into their friends and support systems.

3. Dive Back In: the student needs to invest time and energy in a positive way. They will aim for a pace that suits their personality. Helping the student create organizational tools, lists, and planners to organize their life and activities; showing the student how to divide tasks into smaller portions to avoid procrastination and build a feel good attitude about getting things accomplished or finished; and helping the student to focus on other things like doing something for someone else, all divert the stress into more positive actions.

(Denham 1990)

These skills are interconnected with executive skills development. The capacity to cope with stress is intertwined with the student's capacity for executive functioning—from self-awareness to the thoughtful implementation of stress strategies.

STRESS DIARY-JOURNAL TECHNIQUE

For many individuals, being able to write down their feelings and responses helps them to become more self-aware but also gives them a written record for tracking any type of stress that is occurring. Stress diaries are excellent for tracking short-term stress. Diaries help document events as they happen. Journals can be kept hourly or in half a day or full day formats. The purpose of the journal can provide insight for the student and the adults working with the student to identify the levels of pressure at which the student is operating. Documenting, analyzing, and managing stressors enable the individuals working with the student to do a better job of targeting the sources as well as coming up with suitable interventions.

MENTAL STRESS MANAGEMENT: IMAGERY

Guided imagery is a stress management technique where one uses imagination to picture a person, place, or time that makes one feel relaxed, peaceful, and happy. Calm Place imagery is a technique that relies on all the senses to create and find those relaxing activities that calm the noise in your head or in your body. In using imagery to reduce stress the student must be able to do the following three things: (1) find a quiet space; (2) choose a setting; and (3) relax.

Finding the quiet space is very individual and guiding the student to choose that space is key in helping them feel comfortable enough to close their eyes and breathe slowly and deeply so that they can become calm. What does matter is the student's ability to picture himself in a peaceful environment that has some level of special meaning. This setting is highly personal and should ideally be a space to which the student is emotionally connected. The goal is getting the student immersed in the scene, where he can see, taste, touch and smell—truly experience the sensations of the calm and relaxed place.

How long the student stays in the relaxed scene is up to the adult guiding the process. It is important that when the time is up, the student is able to sit up, have time to float back to reality and process the return to normal daily activities. If time allows, have the student expand on their feelings while they were away in the great calm space. Processing the peacefulness and coping strategies may help the student to tap into those coping skills when in stressful situations (Mindtools 2016).

AFFIRMATIONS: HARNESSING POSITIVE THINKING

Affirmations are positive, specific statements that help an individual overcome self-sabotaging, negative thoughts. They help people visualize and believe and make positive changes to what is happening in their life. Affirmations have been effective in treating people with low self-esteem, depression, anxiety, and a variety of other mental health conditions (Northwestern State University Study). Increasing positive thinking is unlikely to occur on it's own, especially with people who have developed negative thinking habits.

Using Affirmations paired with creative visualizations, journals, and diaries can help the student challenge and overcome negative thinking and self-sabotaging behaviors or cognitive distortions. The challenge is changing the language that is naturally occurring in the student's brain. The adult who is guiding the process might want to have students list all of the negative thoughts that frequently come into their heads.

Once the list is identified, the adult guides the student to switch the negative statement into a positive, present tense statement that the student can repeat frequently when the negative thoughts start to creep in again to counter this negativity. During this process, it is imperative that the affirmation is credible, believable, and based on a realistic assessment of fact. The power of the affirmation lies in the repetition and the timing of its use. Affirmations are more likely to be successful when they are thought or said with feeling and conviction.

PERFECTIONISM: THE PURSUIT OF PERFECT

Perfectionism is a set of self-defeating thought patterns that push students to try to achieve unrealistically high goals. Dr. Tal Ben-Shahar explains that there are two types of perfectionism: adaptive and maladaptive. His research found that adaptive perfectionists work on developing their skills. Their standards are always rising and they approach work with optimism, pleasure and a desire to improve. This is clearly a healthy perfectionism. They see mistakes as an opportunity for growth—as part of the learning process—and willingly accept them as part of their development.

Maladaptive perfectionists are never satisfied with what they achieve. They want everything to be flawless; if not, they dismiss it. Many who have this attitude experience fear of failure, doubt, unhappiness, and painful stressors or emotions. These perfectionists see mistakes as unacceptable, as they believe they will be perceived as incompetent.

Students who are perfectionists become overwhelmed with the demands of schoolwork, social life, and the expectations that are asked of them on a daily basis. According to the *Journal of Counseling and Development* (Mindtools 2016) perfectionism has been linked to health issues such as eating disorders, depression, anxiety, and personality disorders. The quest for perfection can also result in decreased productivity, stress, and troubled relationships.

The Perth Center for Clinical Interventions in Western Australia has developed an approach-model for challenging perfectionist behavior and beliefs. This model directly targets perfectionism but also indirectly targets stress and anxiety that often work in tandem with perfectionism.

1. Identify the behaviors: have the student list everything that they do that must be perfect at school, at home, socially, and with personal relationships.
2. Identify the beliefs: have the students explain why they believe the action must be perfect.
3. Challenge the behavior: have the student come up with one specific step to overcome each behavior.
4. Evaluate the results: once the student has successfully challenged his or her behaviors, have him or her look at what happened, and ask what he or she learned from the experience. The key to success is to challenge one behavior at a time; trying to change all the behaviors becomes overwhelming and students will often become discouraged and revert back to old patterns.

There are many different types of strategies that are effective in dealing with perfectionism tied to anxiety and stress. The goal is to understand the root of the perfectionism and the consequences of all their efforts to be perfect. The following strategies from Mindtools.com can be effective in guiding students to handle the belief and behavior more effectively.

1. Set realistic goals: have student break down the goals in achievable steps.
2. Listen to their emotions: if a student is feeling anxious or stressed, have them reevaluate their goal, question their thoughts about the situation and take actions to slow down and reevaluate their plan of action.
3. Don't fear making a mistake: students need to see that mistakes are part of life, and if taken with the correct perspective, can enrich one's learning experiences and growth. Helping students shift from seeing failure as detrimental to viewing it as an opportunity for development will help the student take risks and seek out new experiences.
4. Readjust the personal rules: students need to understand all the rules or personal expectations that govern their lives on a daily basis. Once the rules have been identified, each rule must be reworded or reworked to become more helpful, flexible, and forgiving. Once this process has been accomplished, the student must practice continuously to affect the thinking patterns behind the perfectionism.
5. Focus on the whole: students must diminish the use of the tunnel vision approach where they focus on one small part of something and ignore the rest. They need to begin looking at a whole first, followed by understanding how each part affects the whole. This approach will enable the student to begin looking at all the positive components that have been accomplished and creatively focus on which part needs additional work or dissection to make it a functioning part of the whole picture.
6. Be aware of internal messages that students use: students need to become more aware of language and internal vocabulary. They need to understand how often they use words like should, must, shouldn't, never, and all, as these words in the inner vocabulary often times create unrealistic expectations and more stress.
7. Relax and be more spontaneous: stressed out students don't stop to relax. The goal here is to have student take regular breaks, walk around, try deep breathing exercises, add spontaneity, and seek out relaxation techniques that help them focus and ground them in the here and now so that they are better able to evaluate and creatively solve the problem that is creating the stress.

Helping students follow the above guidelines enables them to become more self-aware in that they become participants in the treatment, management, or resolution of their stress rather than being the victim of the paralysis that poorly managed stress can create. They become more likely to achieve their goals and dreams and have a much happier and healthy lifestyle.

TOFFLER'S STABILITY ZONES: FINDING PEACE AMONG CHAOS

Toffler defines stability zones as places or things that make you feel safe, relaxed, and secure. They are a buffer, defense, or protection against the outside world. These zones are familiar and safe and do not change; they are predictable and consistent. Stability zones can be things (favorite possessions), people (spouse, best friend, parent), objects (book, souvenir, heirloom) and ideas (religious faith, political ideology, beliefs, values). Students will often have objects as a stability zone. Younger children especially will have a teddy bear, doll, blanket, etc. that is used to help calm themselves down in times of stress. The goal of any stress intervention is to identify ahead of time where this zone is located or what is needed to de-escalate a stressed out student.

Stability zones, if clearly identified by educators, student, and parent in a noncrisis time will lead to more effective communication between all parties when trying to support a student during stressful times. If a student has a behavior support plan, these zones should be clearly stated as well as the process for their use, including under what circumstances the student is allowed to access them.

Clear expectations can prevent acting out behaviors or temper tantrums when the issue can be resolved fairly quickly by having the student access the object, person, place, or prompt that is needed to deescalate or calm the student down. This requires those who interact with the student to be aware of the plan, aware of the student's stress manifestations, aware of what are stress triggers, and aware of student's strategies and prompts. The educator or adult needs to be aware of when to use the prompts and when the student has escalated to needing a different level of support. This also requires staff to be practiced in their own self-management.

TRANSACTIONAL MODEL OF STRESS AND COPING

Richard Lazarus and Susan Folkman (1984) created a model that allows people to identify how to objectively approach the process of accepting and effectively dealing with change. The model has three stages: primary appraisal, secondary appraisal, and coping efforts. In the primary appraisal, the educator-counselor who is working with a student and using this model must evaluate the event and the significance to the student. In so doing one must help the student to see how the change will affect them in a positive or negative way. In breaking down the process, the adult must identify any possible threats or opportunities the change may create. The educator must also identify any risks and positive or negative consequences that might affect the student emotionally.

Once the assessment and analysis has been completed, the educator must help the student identify all of the emotions, both negative and positive, and offer a variety of techniques or strategies to manage these ongoing or new emotions. Students need to become more aware of their thought processes and how they are viewing the new change and managing or not managing their emotions.

The message has to be clearly articulated that not all change is bad and that change can be a positive or a negative experience. If the educator is able to foster a positive attitude through the analysis and an understanding of the impact of the change, the change becomes less scary for the student.

In the secondary appraisal stage, the educator guides students to think about how they can control what is happening with the new change. The educator and student should then look at the resources that they have available to help cope with this change. During this process, they make a list of things that might help the student through the change. An examination of the student's existing skills is done in order to try to figure out what is needed for a successful integration of the new change. If the student is lacking a certain skill set, then decisions need to be made regarding the type of training needed to help the student successfully negotiate the change, and those skills should be taught directly.

The last stage, the coping efforts, addresses the control coping and escape coping strategies. At this stage, the escape coping strategies that the student typically uses are identified and discussed at length. Often times these escape coping strategies are self-destructive or sabotaging to the student. Switching from the escape to the control coping strategies is difficult for many students.

The direct teaching of the strategies and the evaluation of the effectiveness of particular strategies is paramount in helping the student understand what coping skill they are using and whether it is effectively helping them adjust to the change or rather prolonging the agony of having to endure the effects of the change and experiencing a lack of control.

This model is another good example of the common ideas of a cognitive approach—helping children gain insight about the dynamic of gaining immediate relief through impulsive responses to stress resulting sometimes in costly long-term outcomes. The attempt to help children become more cognitively aware through cost-benefit analysis sounds useful for some children.

Victims of trauma, or children with cognitive deficits will need to combine these types of efforts with the creation of environments and supports that provide high levels of external support for stress reduction. This is where many adults get frustrated with some children—the children who have great difficulty with these cognitive approaches because either they are not ready for such an approach or the stress is too great. The unfortunate result of staff frustration is exacerbating the problem via the development of a nonsupportive and stress-increasing relationship.

Through the use of several techniques mentioned throughout this chapter, students can be guided through the process of understanding change, seeing their role in the change and, finally, in accepting what they can do to make the change work for them and the organization or school of which they are a member. During this coaching time, it is important to have students continue to take time out of the day to reflect, eat healthy food, exercise, and de-stress in multiple ways as they work through the process of integrating the new change into their daily lives.

SELF-SABOTAGE AND NEGATIVE SELF-TALK

Negative self-talk comes from a dark place within our minds and bodies. Negative self-talk has been responsible for missed opportunities, suicides, acting out behaviors, miscommunication, and general problems with stress and anxiety. Negative self-talk like "I can't do that", "I'm stupid", "that's too hard" are common in today's classrooms. A level of despair and discouragement is alive and well within the minds of America's students.

The unfortunate aspect of this negative talk is that it comes mostly from internal rather than from external sources. This internal monster rears its ugly head millions of times a day when students are asked to complete a task, explore options, or face a new situation. Negative self-talk is universal—everyone does it. Managing Stress for School success curriculum outlined later in this text presumes that negative thinking is something everyone does so all can gain from self-awareness, turning negative thinking into positive or at least neutral thinking. Negative thinking ranges from normal, everyday self-protective or stress-reducing contemplation or avoidance, to the types of pathological and self-sabotaging levels that are destructive.

Many students do not even realize that they are engaging in negative self-talk, as it is so much part of their daily coping mechanisms. They naturally attribute their lack of success to inadequacy or they blame others. There is often no rational reason for the negative self-talk since quite often the student has the basic ability, skill, and motivation to complete the task (or effectively seek support); they often just get stuck on an obstacle that is blocking their achievement of success. When negative self-talk begins, the added stress of the negative thinking can steer a student away from effective self-regulation.

The student self-sabotages by procrastinating, not pursuing their dreams, worrying, or feeling angry and worthless. They become unable to finish projects, living a life full of dreams, and never accomplishing the steps to achieve the dream. Students can become paralyzed by the worry, anxiety, fear of failing, and self-doubting to the point of never taking a chance and using aggressive rather than assertive communication styles. The end result is a downward spiral that will often lead to depression and erosion of self-confidence and self-esteem.

Breaking the cycle of self-sabotage is outlined in the four-step approach: Recognizing the self-sabotaging behavior, monitoring the negative thinking, challenging the self-sabotaging thinking, and developing self-supporting behaviors (Mindtools 2016).

The first step to help students recognize their self-sabotaging behaviors is to ask a series of questions that enable the student to look at what and how they are thinking. For example; what goals have you had for yourself for a long time and never been able to accomplish? What do you struggle with that you can't understand why? Are you lacking motivation? Are you angry or frustrated a lot and does that cause you to not get things accomplished? Is there something that nags at you every day?

Addressing the questions and analyzing the answers with the student will identify certain negative self-talk patterns or any cognitive distortions that are operating. The goal is to have the student tune in to their self-defeating thinking patterns.

In step two, students are taught how to record and/or write down all the negative thoughts in a journal or a video diary as the behavior is happening or has just happened. If students are too escalated to process at that moment, wait until they have returned to the calm phase and have them do a visual imagery session where they recreate the situation in their mind and talk it through to identify what they were thinking and feeling at that particular moment in time.

Step three is teaching students how to challenge the thinking or the thoughts as they come into their mind. A series of guiding questions can be used: "Is this always true?" "What is really behind my thinking this?" "Are these thoughts rational, or based on clear facts?" "Where is this coming from?" The whole purpose is to have the student challenge and seek evidence to counter the negative thoughts that are leading to self-sabotaging or self-destructive behaviors or actions.

Step four helps students to rebuild their self-confidence, and think more positively or analytically about a situation or a problem. It helps them to identify and defeat the negative thoughts as they come in. Students are guided through questions: "What can I say to myself that is more encouraging or pos-itive?" "What are my options for solving this problem?" "How can I achieve my goal or desire?" "How am I using my assumptions and putting them in a more positive perspective?" "Are my skills, beliefs, and behaviors aligned to help me be successful?" Using this type of questioning will help the student to find a better mental, emotional and physical state to do whatever they set their mind to (Mindtools 2016).

Helping students turn their dreams into reality requires solid planning and effort as well as training, practice, and collegial collaboration and support. They will not change their negative thinking patterns into positive ones without the guidance that helps them believe in themselves and have the confidence to embark on a path toward success. Negative self-talk is a natural direction for many students and breaking the cycle can be a long and arduous journey; however, one is able to get the students to have a greater satisfaction and sense of fulfillment in their lives, which is well worth the effort.

CLASSROOM INTERVENTIONS

The following buffet list of interventions and strategies are meant as a starting point to helping children with anxiety or providing some immediate support to these students. These strategies are not meant as cures but more to manage stress and anxiety in the classroom on a daily basis.

Generalized Anxiety Disorders

1. Give lots of reassurance and genuine, specific praise.
2. Carefully monitor students.
3. Empathize with a student's anxiety.
4. Establish routines and clarify expectations.
5. Allow for a flexible workload.
6. Establish curricula check-in points.
7. Modify instruction for diverse learning styles.
8. Establish provisions for times when students feel overwhelmed (safe or quiet space).
9. Speak with the school counselor, parents, and outside professionals working with the child.

(Cooley 2007)

Obsessive-Compulsive Disorder

1. Reassure student that he or she doesn't have to be perfect.
2. Empathize with student's difficulties.
3. Consider decreasing a student's overall workload.
4. Allow for flexibility in deadlines and testing.

5. Closely monitor student's progress with class work.
6. Avoid grading students on the neatness of work.
7. Create a place where students can calm down when frustrated.
8. Eliminate teasing.
9. If student and family approve, educate your whole class on OCD.

(Cooley 2007)

Social Anxiety Disorder

1. Provide a warm and encouraging environment.
2. Work to improve children's social skills.
3. Foster friendships and joint activities through curriculum.
4. Give high, genuine praise for social behaviors.
5. Show sensitivity when speaking about a socially anxious student.
6. Create a place where overwhelmed students can go to avoid large groups.
7. Give student plenty of time to prepare for class discussion questions.
8. Share or talk about a student's work or contribution.
9. Minimize students' oral reading requirements and oral reports.
10. Speak with others involved in the care and development of the student.

(Cooley 2007)

Post-Traumatic Stress Disorder

1. Create a sense of safety and security in students.
2. Be especially sensitive to a student's background.
3. Provide a safe place for students who become overwhelmed.
4. Modify academic requirements.
5. Create a calm, predictable environment.
6. Speak with the school counselor and parents and other professionals.

(Cooley 2007)

Panic Disorder

1. Respond to a panic attack with reassurance and calming suggestions.
2. Minimize attention from other students.
3. Establish provisions for students experiencing panic (safe or quiet space).
4. Allow for accommodations to address panic and constant worries of an attack.
5. Allow students to be excused from panic-triggering activities and situations.

(Cooley 2007)

School Refusal

1. Eliminate bullying and create safe learning environments.
2. Avoid criticizing students' anxiety.
3. Modify instruction to reach reluctant learners.
4. Adjust classroom expectations.
5. Praise student successes and applaud progress.
6. Build students' social skills.
7. Speak with counselor and parents.

(Cooley 2007)

The above lists of strategies are suggestions and will apply to many different students and situations. I emphasize the need for individual attention based on the specifics of the actual student's difficulty, contextual factors, or triggers occurring for the student.

Strategies, interventions, behavior support plans, and therapeutic counseling plans are all the tools that educators have at their disposal to intervene with students who come to school with anxiety, mood, and other mental health or emotional regulation challenges. Childhood is not a race; it is a journey of experiences that should be filled with inquiry, curiosity, and a sense of calm and peaceful existence.

Life needs to be a journey of self-discovery, experience, and happiness. The only way we will accomplish this is by slowing down, redefining what we consider important, and changing our behavior to maximize the possibilities that a life with less or well-managed anxiety and stress can provide. It is an achievable goal that will need to happen. The path and direction of our existence can be changed with a pair of new lenses that enable us to see the beauty that surrounds and welcomes us daily.

Chapter 7

Personal Journeys

Family Challenges

This chapter reveals insights about the personal journeys that have been experienced by parents and children throughout their school years. As you read the personal heartfelt stories please reflect upon how this journey could have been different for the child and/or family. The goals of including this chapter is for all individuals reading it to become more aware of their abilities to successfully support rather than create more chaos or challenge for these struggling children and adolescents. Awareness can lead to changes in practices and can successfully alter the direction of a child's future. As an educator you can make a difference every time you have a student who is experiencing stress, anxiety, anger, depression, by being compassionate, caring, and empathetic. Enjoy the stories.

AMANDA, AGE TEN (TESTIMONIAL FROM PARENT)

Our daughter absolutely loves school this year 2014–2015. She is eager to learn and adores her fourth grade teacher. She cannot wait to see her classmates each morning, and almost always comes home from school with a big smile on her face excitedly telling us all about her day. She has even made honor roll all quarters this year.

This was not always the case. Last year our daughter had a terrible school year. She almost always came home from school in tears, had few friends, and had poor grades. She also had a teacher who outwardly disliked her—calling her a distraction in front of her peers. Our daughter has ADHD and an anxiety disorder. She is not always easy to work with. We get that. We really do understand.

However, her teacher had no patience for our daughter and was not willing to work with her (or us) to come up with viable solutions. Our daughter would get placed in the back of the room facing the wall during test time so that she would not distract the other students. During other times during the school day she would be placed in the back row of the classroom, furthest away from the teacher, the board, and her classmates. She was often yelled at.

Several times during the school year we would meet with the teacher, guidance counselor, and the special education coordinator hoping to come up with a solution to benefit all involved. Before we had an IEP in place there was little that could be done. The teacher refused to put our daughter in the front of the classroom because she was a "firecracker" and would disturb everyone behind her.

Even with all of the evidence provided that she would do better being seated directly in front of the teacher in her field of vision, she still refused. The teacher wouldn't let our daughter get up for a few minutes to work off some built up energy. Instead, our daughter was made to sit in her seat and squirm.

At recess our daughter would be in tears. Her peers refused to play with her or even be associated with her. She would come home depressed and angry. Her self-esteem was at an all-time low. She felt she was a failure and just didn't want to try anymore. We knew we had to take further steps than just meeting with her teacher. We began the IEP process. With the help of our daughter's pediatrician, her therapist, the school guidance counselor, the special education coordinator, the school psychologist, and her classroom teacher, our daughter began a series of tests and evaluations, and finally an IEP was put into place.

The teacher had no choice but to let our daughter sit in front of the classroom. As it turns out, our daughter wasn't a distraction and started to pay attention more, and began to get better grades. A supportive network was now in place. However, the teacher still had little patience for our daughter . . . we were all happy when the school year came to an end.

We were nervous the first day of school this year. We had no idea what to expect. We were trying to build our daughter's confidence all summer. We were telling her this year it will be different. Our daughter had a brand new, fresh out of college teacher. The first day of school his classroom seating arrangements were a rectangle. There were no front rows, back rows. I knew this year was going to be different. Thankfully, it has been. We haven't had to rely on our daughter's IEP all year. Each student is an individual with individual needs. Our daughter loves school, loves her teacher, and has many friends. It has been a wonderful year.

GRANT, AGE EIGHT (TESTIMONIAL FROM PARENT)

My son, Grant, is eight years old and an only child. Teachers and other adults and peers describe him as bright, kind, thoughtful, and well behaved. He is liked by his peers and is always looking out for the underdog in any situation. He is reserved, a listener, and needs to understand and experience an environment, and its complexity, before he is completely comfortable. Grant reads at a fifth grade level, can multiply and divide, and consistently scores in the 98 percent on standardized tests.

He is tall for his age and has a 504 plan to support his low muscle tone that affects his gross and fine motor muscles. His low muscle tone affects his ability to write legibly. Grant doesn't like large groups of people, loud noises, or unpredictable behavior from others. He prefers to sit in the back of large groups and will remain quiet until he is called on. He almost always answers questions correctly but never freely offers thoughts or ideas to his teachers. When he works with other children in small groups he always allows them to go first to do a task or offers his "share" to them.

Grant attended a home setting for care when he was a young child because my husband and I both work. He began preschool in a Montessori setting at age of three and a half. He had a very hard time at drop off at the start of every school day. He would cling to my husband or me and cry for the first few weeks of school. This continued every year through second grade. In kindergarten the school administrator had to pull him from my husband's leg and carry him into the building. We are told that once he was in his classroom he was fine, but there were days when we would drop him off and hide our own tears as we left him.

This most recent year we have had to change his school setting. Grant was attending the public school system in our town. He was in a second grade class with approximately twenty-five other students. Grant would come home on a daily basis and say that he did nothing all day. We would sit down with him to do homework and he would complete it in less than five minutes. As I looked at the work I realized that it was way below where he was academically.

I waited for two months into the school year before I said anything to the teacher. I wanted to allow her time to assess all of her children and settle into the year. I finally called and asked to set up an appointment with her so we could discuss his academics and see what I could do to help support him at home, and what she and the school could do to help him during the day.

When making the appointment, I made it clear what I wanted to speak about. When I arrived, both she and the principal were present. Both were quiet and looking at me. I started to explain what I had noticed about Grant's academics and asked how we could work together to support him.

The response I received from the teacher addressed very little about my academic concerns for Grant. Instead she began listing "her concerns" about Grant. She stated that he was not academically advanced but was rather demonstrating the following negative behaviors in the class: (1) he doesn't raise his hand in class during discussions; (2) he is often staring into space and looking uninterested (she stated that he was doing that to be rude); and (3) his writing is illegible and he doesn't try his best to be neat.

She insisted that he was doing this to be spiteful because when she reminded him how to hold his pencil he was able to comply. The list continued while the principal and I listened. I was horrified! The forty-five minute meeting didn't address my academic concerns for my son. It did however let me see that she didn't know my child or his learning needs.

Grant began the second grade again that year, in November, at a charter school in town. The school has a Montessori and nature-based philosophy that allows each child to work at their own ability and pace. He is thriving, he loves school, his academic needs are being met, and he is accepted for who he is.

He didn't cry the first day I brought him to his new school; instead, he cried on the last day of school. He had to excuse himself from the final, closing of the year ceremony to "collect himself."

LOUISE (TESTIMONIAL FROM PARENT)

Louise was born in April 1999 weighing ten pounds, sixteen ounces. Her sister who was born before her had colic. I didn't hold her often, because she would scream for hours on end. However, Louise was different. She was a happy and content baby who never fussed or cried. I would cuddle and hold Louise *all* day. Many thought I would spoil her, but I disagreed. I thought there is no such thing as too much love and affection.

The following are doctor's visits and tests that led to Louise's diagnosis. These also include some responses from doctors, therapists, and teachers.

- At six months, we were the parents that banged pots and pans next to Louise to see if we could get a response from her. She would lie on her back and stare at nothing in particular and wouldn't blink an eye when we banged the pots. Louise had her hearing tested at seven months. The results were inconclusive, because she was too young.
- At one and a half years old Louise was not talking. After several doctor's visits and being told she was a late bloomer, Louise began speech therapy in Nashua, New Hampshire. Her in-home play therapy lasted two and a half years and she began to talk. Louise began to talk and was ready to transition into preschool. Her speech pathologist said that our local school

system was notorious for denying special services to students in need. Louise was functioning "okay," but without further support in the school, she would "go backwards." Her S. P. told me to not talk at the IEP meeting and that she would be Louise's advocate. Louise's therapist openly lied about Louise's speech progress and services were granted.

- At four years old, Louise would bang her head against walls, pull her eye lashes out, bite her finger and toe nails until they bled, twirl in circles with her eyes rolled in the back of her head, toe walk, flap her hands, and break down crying in large crowds. The hardest part was Louise would cringe if anyone tried to comfort her with hugs and kisses. It was though it physically hurt her to be touched.

- I approached Louise's case manager with the school district. She told me in order for Louise to receive additional services, I needed to have Louise diagnosed. Following are the steps I took for her to receive services:

1. Louise's physician was not comfortable diagnosing Louise and recommended I take her elsewhere. Louise was diagnosed with Pervasive Personality Disorder by a neurologist in Andover, Massachusetts. The school district would not accept this.

2. Louise was diagnosed with ADHD by a psychologist in Grafton, Massachusetts. The school district would not accept this.

3. The school district suggested I take Louise to a psychiatrist and gave me four contacts. Each office told me Louise was too young to diagnose. I felt totally lost and alone. Louise's world was not a happy one anymore. Louise told me she wished she was dead. A four-year-old should not know this feeling!

4. My husband and I were desperate. I searched the internet with any hospital or clinic that would help Louise. I made many telephone calls over a two week period. Toward the end of the calls, I would try very hard not to cry over the phone.

5. I dialed Tufts Medical Center in Boston. I pleaded (and sobbed) with them to help Louise. The Center for Children with Special Needs at Tufts scheduled Louise for the very next day. Within six months, Louise was diagnosed with Severe ADHD combined type, Sensory Integration Dysfunction, and Expressive Language Disorder. Louise was diagnosed with seven disabilities in her eyes. She wasn't able to control the movement of her eyes. Louise was also hypotonic.

6. The school district scheduled a transition IEP meeting for Louise to enter first grade. I brought the diagnosis with me. I was told the district didn't believe Louise had any of these disabilities and they thought it was emotional. They again suggested I take Louise to counseling. True story!

7. We owned a vacation home in the White Mountains. I went home and telephoned the SAU and enrolled my girls into the local elementary school.

8. The Special Education Team at this school told me that many parents complain that other schools don't provide services for their children, but when they read Louise's IEP for first grade . . . they were shocked the previous school district gave Louise a marker to write with. She couldn't hold a pen or pencil. This new school tied a pencil to her hand with elastics. They provided a speech pathologist, occupational therapy, and an aide.

9. Louise did great until fifth grade. Her teacher was not following the IEP. At several meetings, she offered her opinion that Louise was simply rude and didn't feel the need for her to have extra help. I sent a letter to the Special Ed Director at the SAU stating the teacher was violating Louise's civil rights and explained how. The director held a meeting with the team and apologized for the teacher's behavior. It was March and the IEP was finally being followed.

10. Louise had a project in English that was due after her April vacation. She chose to read the book *The Boy in the Striped Pajamas*. Louise read the book several times and rented the movie from the library. She spent her entire vacation writing an essay and creating a poster about the story. Louise was passionate and felt a lot of compassion for the boy. Then her heart broke. Louise received a D for a mark for the report. Louise's IEP stated she was to have any projects or essays in English reviewed by her aide for corrections. When I asked Louise if her aide assisted, she replied no. I contacted her aide. Then her teacher. Then her case manager. Then the principal. I wanted her grade to reflect a mark consistent with receiving her support as stated in her IEP. Louise's grade was changed to a B. This began in April and ended the last week in May. But it was too late. The B didn't matter to Louise because she didn't feel like she mattered.

These stories happened off and on for most of Louise's school years. As her parents, we had to be a constant advocate for her. As Louise matures, we have taught her to have a voice and to be her own advocate. We were honest with her about her disabilities and included her on making some decisions in her own IEP. This empowered her to seek help when we weren't able to be there.

Louise is a junior in high school. She recently tested a one hundred and twenty-eight in an IQ test for her re-evaluation for services. Although Louise is "superior" to her classmates in intelligence, she still says there must be something wrong with the test. Louise now experiences panic attacks. She isn't sure why she has them and now is seeking help for them. This is her next hurdle, but Louise has always communicated with us and I know she will conquer this.

High school has been good to Louise. Her case manager uses Louise as an example to other students who need to advocate for themselves. Last week, Louise was inducted into the NH Technology Honors Society. She is studying her third language, Latin. Louise feels she will be able to learn more languages more easily if she studies Latin. She wants to study international commerce or become a stock broker.

In conclusion, these are only three stories of thousands of parents and children who suffer because of the educational system's inability to be aware of the challenges of anxiety and other existing conditions. It is not completely the fault of the educators because many are not trained to understand mental health issues, and they do the best they can. In reading these stories it is my hope that the next time you have a student like this in your classrooms you will be aware and take the steps needed to support both the child and the family.

Part II

MANAGING STRESS FOR SCHOOL SUCCESS

Curriculum Framework

Small and Whole Group Lessons

Eric Mann

Managing Stress for School Success (MS[3]) is a stress awareness and stress management strategy. It is designed as a supportive, insight-oriented prevention strategy for behavioral concerns. When implemented with fidelity and diligence, it can provide a preemptive approach to behavioral repetition or emotional escalation, and can be a tool for promoting self-awareness and emotional self-regulation. As a universal school-wide strategy, MS[3] provides a common language and framework for addressing and understanding concerning behavior via a stress paradigm.

How will MS[3] help students? Perceptions generate thoughts, which lead to feelings, ultimately resulting in behaviors. Since stress impacts our perceptions, it follows that learning how to better manage stress will lead us to better, more thoughtful behavioral outcomes. Improved awareness of one's own stress triggers and one's unique manifestations of stress can lead to improved self-regulation. With correct implementation, MS[3] supports children and adults to feel in better control of their thoughts and feelings, and therefore, in better position to make conscious behavioral choices that are self-helping and goal supporting, rather than self or goal defeating.

Stress can also significantly impact executive functioning regardless of the strength or weakness of a student's, or staff member's, baseline executive skills. Poorly managed stress decreases, or compromises, executive functioning, which leads to rigid or impulsive responses and behaviors. Impulsive reactions (either by student or adult) often set the stage for conflict or crisis.

MS[3] uses well-researched strategies for stress awareness and stress management and builds upon principles embedded in Cognitive Behavioral Therapy (CBT), functional behavioral analysis, and Life Space Crisis Intervention (LSCI). The curricula are organized by lessons and/or sessions.

Each individual lesson is set up in a user-friendly format for educators to follow and progress.

There are two curriculum frameworks: one designed for whole class or advisory instruction and one that is geared toward small group instruction that can be incorporated as a "Tier Two" intervention in a Response to Intervention Behavioral (RtI) continuum. The whole group framework has a level of generalization that can be tailored to the individual needs of the classroom and the particular grouping of students (3–6). The small group curriculum is meant to be followed more systematically and may progress at a slower pace due to the challenges that students may have as they learn and practice new skills.

SMALL GROUP INSTRUCTION FRAMEWORK

The small group curriculum was designed for more individualized and time-intensive work with students who will benefit from more focused teaching and a higher level of attentiveness to each student's challenges in identifying and managing stress. Thoughtful development of post-group routines (i.e., once the group sessions have been taught) that strengthen and solidify the learning are important to maximize the benefits of the group curriculum. MS^3 for small groups is designed for small groups of students who are able to work effectively with others and who stand a reasonable chance of benefiting from the course.

To maximize the potential benefits, it is important that what is learned in the small group is practiced in the "real world" of the student's school day. Therefore, it is important that all who interact with the students are aware of how to support MS^3 skills throughout the student's school day. MS^3 lessons should not be taught in isolation, that is, without the systematic support of a team of adults. Prompts, pre-corrections, supportive corrections, positive feedback, and validating reflections will serve to increase practice opportunities and increase the likelihood of student insights pertaining to the benefits using the strategies.

MS^3 may be helpful with children with emotional and behavioral disorders; however, careful selection of group membership or the option to implement or enhance the curriculum individually may be necessary. In addition, implementation with children with significant emotional or behavioral challenges requires highly qualified and talented facilitators to build rapport effectively and to handle the potentially complex group dynamics and personal issues that may arise.

It is important to establish a "trust agreement" *prior* to the start of group. Individually, discuss the purpose of the course and why trust is important.

Include the following elements in the trust agreement and respectfully seek the student's consideration and signature:

- *To establish a group in which all members of the group feel comfortable talking about personal things, I agree to support and understand rather than make fun of or, in any way, put down anyone's comments. I agree that whatever is said during group remains in the group. Nothing that is said during group sessions about a person's likes, dislikes, thoughts, opinions or feelings should be repeated to anyone outside the group.*

This curriculum may be facilitated by a single facilitator or co-led by two facilitators. If co-led, it is recommended that both facilitators are present at every session. It is recommended that facilitators plan ahead in order to avoid common barriers to full implementation and to plan for enough time for each session (note: sessions may be broken up into smaller segments at the discretion of the facilitator[s]). Ensure contingency plans are in place so that facilitators are not called out for crises during planned group time. Also, ensure contingency plans for student or facilitator absence. Gain classroom teacher commitment to prioritize the group if group sessions are scheduled to occur during instructional time (i.e., establish teacher commitment to the value of the group toward long-term academic, behavioral, and social outcomes).

Each session is organized as follows: (1) "Big Messages for this Session." This section describes the important ideas to be conveyed in the session. (2) "Group Instruction or Discussions." These sections contain instruction of new ideas or precede or prompt discussions. (3) "Activity" sections provide instructions for related activities.

Some sessions will prompt optional activities (used at facilitator discretion) or recommend activities to occur in between sessions. Implementing each session with fidelity is important. Ensure that sessions are not missed or short-changed due to systems barriers or scheduling so that each student receives the full breadth of the course.

Small Group Lessons

LESSON 1

SMALL GROUP INSTRUCTION FIGURES	
Session 1: Opening and Everyone Has Stress **(May Take 2-3 Thirty-Minute Sessions to Complete)**	

Big Messages for this Session	*Prior to the start of the group, the group leader should review the MS3 Survey in Appendix and consider whether to use or adapt this survey for pre-post information that may help to assess the value or effectiveness of this course.*
	 1. This group is mainly about three things:
	   a. Awareness of Stress
	   b. Managing Stress
	   c. Gaining insights about link between managing stress and goal-supporting behavior.
	 2. Everyone has stuff that happens in life that causes stress.
	 3. Stress sometimes motivates people in positive ways.
	 4. Stress sometimes leads to frustration, aggression, worries or giving up.
	 5. A small problem can lead to a bigger problem if it isn't well-managed when it's small.
	 6. Things that stress *you* may not stress someone else; things that stress others may not stress you.

Organizing the Group	Say: • Welcome! We'll be meeting (state frequency) to complete a course together on stress awareness and stress management. • We'll get to know a lot about each other during our time together. • We'll learn about stress, and we'll learn about how and why it's important to manage stress. • *Most of it will be easy and fun.* • There will be a lot of group discussions and group activities. • We may talk about personal things, so we need to agree that what gets discussed here, stays here. It's not OK to talk outside the group about what is said here. That trust is important. • Here are the trust agreements you signed when you agreed to be part of this group (hand back copies of individual confidentiality agreements signed by each group member). • Also, we need to make some quick rules about respectful discussions. Let's do this together: • What are some good rules for having respectful discussions? Guide group to include these norms for discussions: • One person talks at a time; Stay on topic; Stay positive with each other; Avoid put-downs; What gets said here, stays here; Other...?
Discussion: What is Stress?	Say: 1. Things happen in life that cause a person to feel stress. 2. *Stress* can be defined or understood as <u>*anything that uses up mental or physical energy*</u>. So when we have a lot of stress it can be harder to be at our best (as a worker, as a student, as a friend). ○ (It may be useful to provide a visual to demonstrate how stress uses up mental or physical energy sometimes leaving less energy (or personal resources) to do your best. Example: show

	an image of a brain with low stress – all areas are able to function fully to complete work and social tasks. Then show a brain cluttered by stressful thoughts. There is less brain available for all the work and social tasks that are expected).
	
	 3. Everyone has stress.
	
	 Prompt Discussions:
	 • What is your understanding of "Stress"?
	      o Validate students' understanding of Stress while helping to clarify.
	 • Some people say they are "stressed-out" when they feel overloaded or overwhelmed, when they have a lot to deal with, or when they feel "pressure".
	      o Have you ever heard the expression "stressed out"? When have you heard it or used it? What does "Stressed Out" mean?

Discussion: Managing Stress	• Sometimes people *manage* their stress -- they handle it -- and it doesn't stop them from achieving the things that matter to them, but... • Sometimes stress causes a person to quit/give up, walk-out, shut-down, or get aggressive. • Stress could also lead a person to feel depressed, angry or worried. o *Have you ever reacted, or seen someone react, to stress in any of these ways?* • These kinds of reactions to stress usually don't *solve problems*. • Sometimes these reactions can make a small problem bigger, or cause new problems. *Prompt group responses to the following examples:* • School example: It might be a relief to say "I'm done, I'm not working anymore!" when a teacher tells you to try harder or work faster. Deciding to be done may feel like a relief at first, but then not getting the work done might lead to other problems. • Work example: It might be a relief to say "I Quit!" if your boss at work is being a jerk and is on your case. Quitting may feel good for a moment or two—it may be a relief --but then you realize that you don't have a job but you still need to buy food and pay the rent. • If someone is annoying you while you are trying to think about something, it might stop the person by yelling at them to get away, or even physically pushing them away. But you might realize later that yelling at them or pushing them caused bigger problems. • *Do you know any other examples of someone making an impulsive decision that might feel good in the moment but might cause a bigger problem later on?*
Activity: Visible List of Group's Stressors	• Things that bother or stress *you* might not bother or stress someone else. • Things that stress *someone else* might not bother you and may be easy for you manage. *Prompt group response to the question:* • What stresses you (i.e., what triggers stress)? *If more prompting is needed, say:* • Who can name something that bothers you; something that makes you feel angry, bummed out, frustrated, annoyed, or worried? • *Make a visible list of the group's stated stressors:*

	○ *NOTE: KEEP THIS STRESS LIST FOR THE ACTIVITY BELOW* ○ Continue prompting until there are at least 10 stressors listed. ○ *Suggestion:* Group facilitator should share one (or more, if needed to prompt the group) of his/her own stress triggers and include that stressor on the visible list. *Say:* • Is there anything on the list that stresses someone else but doesn't stress you? • Is there anything on the list that stresses you but doesn't seem to stress others?

Optional Activity: Emotional Connections	• On chart paper prepare a section/area for each of these five 'feeling' statements:
	    Makes me mad/angry Makes me sad
	    Makes me frustrated/aggravated/annoyed
	    Makes me worried/nervous/uncomfortable
	    Makes me embarrassed/self-conscious
	• Read through the 'stress list' that was created during the last discussion:
	• Ask the group to place each stress trigger with the feeling it causes.
	Encourage the group to match every stressor to a feeling. For example:
	• *Stress Trigger:* "I hate it when my brother tries to get me in trouble," the facilitator asks, "What section would you put this in?"
	• *Stressor Trigger:* "I don't like when I have to read in front of the class," the facilitator might prompt "Lots of kids feel nervous or maybe a little self-conscious when that happens – how does it make you feel?"
	• If a student names a feeling that is not labeled, add a section for that feeling.
	• Encourage awareness that stress causes different feelings for different people.
	When all of the stressors have been matched to a feeling, say:
	• Look at all these *real* stressors and *real* feelings.
	• Some of these stressors may not be a big deal to you, but to others, could be a really big deal.
	• Sometimes stressors add up. Something that might not have bothered you yesterday might bother you more today *because you have other stressors too.*

(Optional) Discussion Prompts: Examples of When Stress Does and Doesn't Stop a Person from Achieving Goals	*Read the following examples of when stress does NOT stop a person from achieving their goals and discuss reactions:* 1. It's a tie game (baseball) and it's up to me to get a hit – the pressure is on but my focus and determination are at the highest level. 2. My house is a mess and mom will be home in 10 minutes – I work like crazy to get everything neat and in place. 3. I see my 3-year old sister about to walk under a dangling tree branch – I get her out of the way so quickly that I can't believe how fast I am. *Read the following examples of when stress is overwhelming and <u>DOES</u> stop a person from achieving their goals and discuss reactions:* 1. I have a lot of homework. I hate homework!! I don't know why they have to give homework every stinkin' night. I don't even know what to do. The heck with it. I'm done!
	2. I'm in a fight with my friend and I am going to see her on the bus this morning. I am SO mad at her that I spaced out and forgot to bring my money that is due today for the field trip. If *ANYONE* messes with me this morning they'll be sorry. 3. My dad left for Afghanistan (army deployment) this weekend. My mom is all nervous and sad. She cried all night. This morning she forgot to get me up in time for school. There was no time to shower or to brush my hair. I got mad at her and she yelled at me. When I got to school I didn't talk to anyone. I went right to my desk and put my head down. I am doing *nothing* today. • I bought a new shirt yesterday and wore it today. Some kids made fun of it on the bus. I thought it was a cool shirt but I guess it's stupid. I won't wear that stupid shirt again! During reading today, my teacher asked me to come up to read something I wrote. I said "No". She asked again and I yelled "NO!" She made me sit in the hall for being "rude". What a jerk!

LESSON 2

	Session 2: Reacting to Stress – PART 1
	Two Ways People React to Stress

Big Messages for this Session	1. Goal-supporting behaviors are behaviors that help a person reach his/her goals (*achieve things that matter to you*).
	2. Goal-defeating behaviors are behaviors that push a person further away from his/her goals (*further from things that matter to you*).
	3. When a person manages (handles) stress well, goal-supporting behavior is more likely.
	4. There are two general ways that people respond to stress:
	   a. They *behave without thinking* (they act impulsively).
	   b. They use Stress Management to *manage* the stress.
	5. Impulsive responses to stress often result in goal-defeating behaviors (behaviors that may have immediate benefit, but have long-term cost).
	6. *Managing* the stress is usually the best way to produce goal-supporting behaviors (this may be harder to do in moment but usually has both short and long-term benefits).

Instruction: Impulsivity	*Say:* • Let's discuss *"Goal-Supporting Behavior"*: • Some behaviors help a person to reach/achieve his/her goals. These behaviors are Goal-Supporting Behaviors (behaviors that *help you to achieve things that matter to you*). • Goal-supporting behaviors help a person achieve personal goals or accomplish things that matter. They may lead to building good relationships and friendships. They may help a person with their learning, or with growing up, or handling life's challenges. o Ask for examples (practicing guitar, baseball or dancing; being kind to a person you want to be friends with; getting homework done if good grades matters to you...) • Goal-supporting behaviors are more likely to happen when a person manages stress well.
	• Now let's discuss *"Goal-Defeating Behavior"*: • Some behaviors lead a person further from his/her goals. These are Goal-defeating Behaviors (behaviors that lead you away from accomplishing things that matter to you). • Goal-defeating behaviors often happen when a person acts *impulsively* to deal with stress. o Ask for examples (refer to discussions from last session). • Sometimes impulsive behaviors have short-term *benefits* (they solve an immediate problem; get some quick relief), but they often cause long-term *costs* (problems later on). • When a person really learns to manage stress, they realize that it's possible to feel better in the moment *AND* still accomplish what matters.

Instruction: "The Two Ways"	*Create a 'Two Ways People Deal with Stress' poster visible so you can point to it as you speak, or, have Group Members create a "Two Ways People Deal with Stress" Poster (after instruction and discussion). Say:*
	
	• One way people respond to stress is to "Behave (or act) without thinking" – they show what they feel through behavior without thinking. Another word for this is *impulsive*.
	   ○ If I am angry, I might scream, hit, or throw something, or storm away.
	   ○ If I am frustrated, I might quit what I am doing and give up.
	   ○ If I am worried about something I might walk away, not try, or I might try to pretend that nothing's wrong but avoid dealing with the problem.
	   ○ If I am sad, I might neglect my health or give up on a friendship.
	   ○ Behaving without thinking things through usually doesn't solve the problem or take away the stress, and it could result in bigger problems.
	• *Another way people respond to stress is to "Manage it"* -- This is usually the healthiest and most effective way to respond to stress: Managing stress means you are really handling the stress. Managing stress means that you accept how you are feeling (it's fine to feel sad or angry or frustrated) but then you figure out a way to manage things so you can still be successful (i.e., achieve things that matter to you).
	• *Managing* your stress is '*goal-supporting*', because it helps settle your feelings which leads you to behaviors that help you achieve your goals.
	• *Behaving without Thinking*, or acting impulsively, may be '*goal-defeating*' because difficult feelings can continue or may get worse (or bigger). Goal-defeating behaviors can end up creating even more stress.
	• Point to (or create) the '2 Ways to Deal with Problems or Feelings' Poster.
	• Tell them that this poster will always be visible in this room as a reminder.

Activity: "Two Ways"	*Set up chart paper with the following two categories:* Behave (act) without thinking (Impulsive) Manage the stress *Prompt to share examples of the 2 ways people deal with stress and record on chart paper:* 1. *When you've Behaved (Acted) Without Thinking (behaved impulsively).* Students share examples of
	when they or others have acted on their feelings without thinking. *Prompts that may help:* • Have you ever seen someone take out their problems and feelings on others (siblings, parents, teacher, friends...)? ○ Example: Being mad at your brother, but then being mean to someone else. • Have you ever been yelled at for nothing (no good reason) by someone who is in a bad mood (have you ever done that to someone)? • Did you ever see someone quit quickly because they got frustrated? • Did you ever observe someone suddenly rip up a paper or run off? Did you ever wonder about the stress the person might be feeling? 2. *When you've Managed your Stress.* Students share examples of when they have managed stress. This may be more difficult for students to recall. *Prompts that may help:* • Can you think of a time when something was bothering you and you talked it out with someone? • Can you think of a time when you were angry and you used words to solve it rather than getting physical or screaming or taking it out on someone or something? • Can you think of a time when you were frustrated and said to yourself, "I know this is frustrating but giving up isn't going to help me"? • Can you think of a time when you were excited about something and you realized that you had too much energy, and rather than let the extra energy get you into misbehavior, you told an adult you needed to take a walk to get some of the energy out?

LESSON 3

	Session 3: Reacting to Stress – PART 2: *Thoughts, Feelings and Behavior*
Big Messages	1. It is our thoughts that cause situations to be stressful. 2. Feelings are reactions to our thoughts. 3. Behaviors are reactions to our feelings.
Discussion: Thoughts to Feelings to Behavior	*Say:* • Thoughts lead to feelings. • Feelings lead to behavior. • This is true for people of all ages: adults and children. *Prompt Discussion:* • Think about a problem or stressor like doing homework. • What thoughts do you have and what feelings start because of your thoughts? *Prompt if needed:* • Let's say your thoughts are something like: I hate math; I don't see the point of this; I don't even

	know what to do; I can't believe I have to do this instead of playing my video game or listening to music....
	• Now, what feelings happen?
	   o Note: It may be helpful to show a feelings list or feelings chart in addition creating a "What Stresses You?" poster. The pictures represent feelings that emerge when people are faced with stressful situations.
	  • What picture reminds you of how you react when you are stressed? Do any of the pictures remind you of other people when they are stressed? Think about your own behavior when you are feeling stressed out. Think of the math example above, what behaviors might happen as a result of the feelings?

	Note: choose one example to use for this activity. If time allows, do a second example. On chart paper, draw three circle graphs (see activity sheet example below) for the following examples (One circle each): 1. Stress, 2. Thoughts & Feelings and 3. Behavior: Sherri's Stress Sherri's Thoughts & Feelings Sherri's Behavior

Activity	After reading an example below, prompt the group: 1. *What stress, thoughts & feelings, and behaviors did the person in the example have?* 2. *Post responses in the appropriate place on the circle graphs (in the open part of the circles around the names).* Example 1: Sherri thinks she is terrible at math – in fact, she believes she's worse at math than anyone. Last night she didn't sleep well and this morning her best friend Shawna is absent from school. She is given a math worksheet at 9:30 during math class. She starts the worksheet but feels stressed and frustrated. She thinks her peers all can do the worksheet easily, and thinks she is getting all the problems wrong. She is sure she must be stupid. Sherri starts to feel frustrated, sad and even mad at herself -- and she even feels mad at her teacher. She puts her pencil down and puts her head on the desk. When the teacher asks her to get to work, she ignores her teacher. Example 2: Ted hits Paul hard in the arm after Paul accidentally bumps him on the way to the bookcase at the beginning of silent reading time. Ted is sent to the office and Ted tells the assistant principal that Paul is a jerk -- he is sure that Paul bumped into him on purpose. Later, Ted's teacher meets with him to talk. Ted tells her that an older boy told him on the bus this morning that he was going to beat him up bad after school.
Discussion	*Lead the group in a discussion about linkages between thoughts, feelings and behavior:* • *Encourage this insight:*
	o By having more control of thinking, we can impact our feelings. And if we can impact our feelings, we can be more in control of our behavior.

LESSON 4

Session 4: Self-Talk and Your Mood
(How Positive and Negative Thinking can Change Your Mood/Feelings)

Big Messages for this Session	1. Self-talk is something almost everyone does. It happens when we are thinking to ourselves.
	2. Some self-talk is negative. It can bring you down and lead to feeling sad, mad or discouraged.
	3. Some self-talk is positive and can lift you up and lead to feeling hopeful and more confident.
	4. Negative self-talk, or *negative thinking*, can cause stress.
	5. Negative thinking can be goal-defeating because it can lead to big feelings.
	6. Positive self-talk, or *positive thinking*, can reduce stress.
	7. Positive thinking is a stress management strategy.
	8. You have the power to change your own mood/feelings with positive self-talk.
Discussion: Positive and Negative Thinking	Write the words "Negative Thinking", "Positive Thinking" and "Mood/Feelings" on the board. Refer to these words as you discuss:
	• 'Self-talk' happens when you think to yourself or talk out loud to yourself.
	• *Everyone* uses self-talk.
	• 'Negative Thinking' is a type of self-talk that brings you down or makes you feel discouraged. Here are examples of negative thoughts:
	○ "This work is too hard."
	○ "Everyone must be smarter than me."
	○ "That kid doesn't like me."
	○ "I'm terrible at this. I know I am going to fail."
	○ "I may as well not try."
	○ "Everyone thinks my hair looks stupid today."
	• 'Positive Thinking' is self-talk that can lift you up and make you feel encouraged or confident:
	- "I can handle anything."
	- "Even if I get something wrong or make a mistake it can't stop me."
	Discuss:
	• Who in this group does self-talk?
	• Who does negative thinking? What negative thoughts do you have?
	• Who does positive thinking? What positive thoughts do you have?
	• Are you more of a negative thinker or positive thinker (a pessimist or an optimist)?

Discussion: Mood	*Say:*
	
	• 'Mood' is a word that refers to the way you are feeling.
	
	• *Self-talk* can have a strong influence on your mood or feelings:
	
	    ○ Negative thinking is usually goal-defeating because it can put a person in a mood that feels sad, frustrated, angry, nervous, ashamed or discouraged.
	
	    ○ Positive thinking can create a mood that feels happy, confident, hopeful or optimistic.
	
	• You can have control over your mood -- by controlling whether you are doing negative thinking or positive thinking!
	
	• What type of mood are you in right now? Think about it.
	
	• Did you ever notice that when you have lots of stress or you are in a bad mood, you do more negative thinking?

Activity: Start a Positive Thinking Journal	*Note: Below is an activity to develop a Positive Thinking Journal (PTJ). PTJ is a stress management strategy. This strategy is useful for some, but not for everyone. Be mindful of your group of students. If it doesn't seem like a useful strategy for this group, consider other ways to help the students learn how to:* • *Start each day (or each new activity, etc.) with positive thinking (being proactive).* • *Recognize when negative thinking is happening.* • *Replace negative thinking with positive thinking.* 1. Provide group members with a small blank booklet and have each of them begin a 'Positive Thinking Journal' (PTJ). The PTJ is a place for each group member to record positive thoughts, drawings or pictures (anything that can be placed in the journal). 2. Using a PTJ is a *stress management strategy.* You can use it when negative thinking affects your mood. You can use it to help start each day or each new activity with a positive attitude. 3. Reading positive words or ideas, or looking at comforting or inspirational pictures or drawings, can help turn a negative mood into a positive mood. 4. Give students 5 minutes to place in their PTJ anything (words, ideas, drawings, pictures, etc.) that could help build a positive (good) mood. • Prompt students to enter things that bring a smile or boost energy (provide a word list if helpful). • Prompt to write important dates or special days or activities to look forward to. • Prompt to draw pictures of important things, important people, important pets, etc. that might cause positive thoughts (if they aren't comfortable with drawing, they can name the people, pets, etc. and plan to get actual pictures to paste in the PTJ...).

- Prompt to write words that might inspire positive thoughts or feelings. Words like: "Confidence"; "Self-Control"; "Strength"; "Success"; "Resilience"; "Determination".
- Write a favorite saying or expression that gives you a positive outlook or makes you laugh:
    - "Embrace Life"; "If at first you don't succeed…"
    - "To create more positive results in your life, replace "If Only" with "Next Time".
    - "It is only those who never do anything who never make mistakes".
    - "A positive attitude may not solve all your problems, but it will annoy enough people to make it worth the effort".

5. After 5 minutes ask students to share some of the positive thoughts that they have written (or drawn or paste) in their positive thinking journal.

6. Encourage students to record new positive thoughts in their PTJ that they hear from others.

7. Provide 10 minutes for students to:

    a. Continue to write down (or draw) any positive thoughts or ideas.

    b. Decorate their PTJ.

    c. Decide the best place to keep their PTJ.

8. Tell students that they can add thoughts to their PTJ at any time.

    a. The facilitator should plan a minute during each remaining session to add to the PTJ.

- Tell students that using a positive thinking journal is one example of a "Stress Management Strategy" that they can use any time stress is building up or negative thinking is starting.
- This is a *stress management strategy* because it helps a person manage the impact of stress.

LESSON 5

	Session 5A: Types of Negative Thinking: Discounting the Positive and Mind-Reading (LSCI Institute) *Note: Session 5B covers 2 additional types of negative thinking: Dwelling and Awfulizing. You may consider 5B optional or you may decide to briefly cover all 4 types.*
Big Messages for this Lesson	1. *'Discounting the Positive'* is a type of negative thinking. 2. *'Negative Mind-Reading'* is a type of negative thinking. 3. *'Discounting the Positive'* and *'Negative Mind-Reading'* can be goal-defeating. 4. Everyone (including adults) discounts the positive sometimes, and some people do it a lot. 5. Everyone mind-reads sometimes, and some people do it a lot. 6. When a person does a lot of negative thinking, it can lead to negative feelings, bad mood, and goal-defeating behaviors.

Discussion: Discounting the Positive	*Say:*
	• *Discounting the Positive* is a type of Negative Thinking. It happens when a person ignores everything positive and only thinks about the negative.
	• Almost everyone *Discounts the Positive* sometimes; some people do it a lot.
	• Imagine thoughts you have after receiving a compliment -- like if someone says "you are a really good sister or brother"; or "you drew an amazing picture"; or "you have a nice smile"; or "you have really good taste in clothes".
	• You may have positive thoughts after a compliment: "Yeah, I guess I am a good sister".
	• But, you also could respond to a compliment with negative thoughts: "You should see me when I am mean to my little brother" or "My smile shows my big teeth and I look stupid" or "Other people dress better than me".
	• Remember, stress takes up your mental energy, and negative thinking increases stress.
	• You may respond to a compliment by discounting it -- and turning it into a negative.
	• This is called *Discounting the Positive!!*
	• Discounting the positive adds to a person's stress. Negative thinking can lead to a bad mood.
	• Bad mood or negative feelings often lead to goal-defeating behaviors.
	Ask:
	• Do you ever discount the positive?
	• What are examples of when you've discounted the positive?
	• Examples to prompt discussion: How might a person discount the positive in these circumstances:
	   ○ You get a test back from a teacher and you got 19 out of 20 questions correct;
	   ○ You have 3 good friends who like you a lot, but one of them got mad at you today.

Discussion: Mind-Reading	*Say:* • Now let's talk about another type of thinking called *Mind-reading*. • Mind-reading is something that almost everyone does. • Do you ever think that you know what someone else is thinking? • Do you ever predict/guess that someone will be unfair, unhelpful or unkind? • Do you ever think that someone is thinking something bad or negative about you?

	• These are all examples of negative 'Mind-Reading'.
	• Sometimes a person 'jumps to conclusions' based on mind-reading.
	• 'Jumping to conclusions' is when a person makes a very quick decision based on only a small amount of information.
	• Jumping to conclusion can lead you down the wrong road to goal-defeating behavior.
	Say:
	• The most important thing to know about mind-reading is this:
	    When a person mind-reads, sometimes they are correct (or partly correct),
	    but sometimes they are just plain wrong.
	Ask:
	• Do you ever do mind-reading or notice that someone else is mind-reading?
	    o What are some examples?
	• Have you ever heard someone say anything like?:
	• "I didn't ask Melanie to go to the mall with me because I knew she'd say 'no'"
	• "I never go to the after school club because all the kids in that club hate me"
	• "My teacher thinks I am a bad kid and is always watching me"
	• "When I walked into my classroom today everyone thought my new haircut looks stupid"
	• Notice -- I didn't say these statements are never true - they *could* be true! But when we mind-read, we jump to wrong conclusions since we don't have all the information to know for sure.
	Prompt a discussion using the mind-reading examples above:
	• Let's look at how mind-reading and jumping to conclusions can lead to goal-defeating results:
	• Look at the first example (about "Melanie"), *maybe the person is correct...but maybe not*. If she is not correct, she may have lost an opportunity to have a friend join her at the mall. Because of her negative mind-reading and jumping to conclusions, she never asks.
	• In the next example, the student thinks all kids in the club hate her so she decides not to attend the club meeting – even though she wants to. Her thinking keeps her from trying. It *is* possible that the girls in the club really don't like her and will be mean to her. But, it's also possible that the girls will be nice and maybe if they get to know her, they'll be more comfortable together.
	• In the last example, a boy thinks his teacher thinks he is a 'bad' kid and wants to punish him. It *could* be true. But, it is possible that the teacher has many thoughts about him – and maybe some of them are very positive. But since he *thinks* the teacher thinks he is 'bad', he may decide to misbehave just to get back at the teacher.
	• In the next example, a boy has the idea that everyone is thinking about his hair. It is possible kids *are* thinking about his hair. But it is possible that classmates haven't even noticed -- some might even like it. Maybe some don't like it but think it's interesting (rather than bad or ugly). As a result of mind-reading, the boy may feel grumpy, irritated, or mad. He may take a bad mood out on someone. Has he 'jumped to conclusions'?
	• When you mind-read and jump to conclusions, your thoughts may not be correct and you might end up with goal-defeating behavior.

	• Don't let mind-reading stop you from achieving your goals.
Activity	Using a Positive Thinking Journal (PTJ) can remind you not to discount the positive or to mind-read. When you catch yourself discounting the positive or doing negative mind-reading, try looking at your PTJ and replac your negative thinking with positive thinking. Take a minute to add any new ideas to your Positive Thinking Journal.

	Session 5B: Types of Negative Thinking (optional): Dwelling and Awfulizing (*Making a Mountain out of a Molehill*)
Big Messages for this Lesson	1. Dwelling and Awfulizing are 2 types of negative thinking that almost everyone does. 2. When you dwell, you get stuck on a negative thought and can't stop thinking about it. 3. Dwelling can bring you down, reduce your energy, or lead to angry feelings. 4. Dwelling can lead to goal-defeating behavior. 5. Awfulizing is when you make a bigger deal out of something than it needs to be or make something much worse than it has to be. 6. Both Dwelling and Awfulizing add stress because negative thinking leads to bigger feelings (sadness, anger, anxiety,…) and takes up your mental energy.
Discussion: Dwelling	*Say:* • Do you ever lie on your bed, sit on the couch, or sit at your desk and think about something over and over? • It might be something you said or something you did; it keeps replaying in your mind. • It might be something that you are worried about. • It might be about something you are not looking forward to or dreading. • It might be something someone else said/did that bothered you. • When you do any of these things, you are Dwelling. • The problem with dwelling is that it leads to negative feelings and a bad mood. • Dwelling almost never focuses on a solution; you just replay the problem over and over and your feelings stay (or get more) sad, mad, frustrated, worried… Here is an example of Dwelling to discuss: *Rhonda met the new the girl and asked why her family moved here. The girl paused, looked down, and said, "I don't want to talk about it." All night Rhonda kept thinking about it. Sometimes she felt a little mad at the girl; sometimes she felt stupid for asking the question; other times she wished she hadn't spoken to her at all. In the morning she was a little sad, a little mad, and very tired.* Another Dwelling example to discuss: *Bill has football tryouts next week. He can't stop thinking about it. He hates tryouts – he always thinks he plays worse in tryouts than in real games. He wishes he could skip tryouts and just be on the team. Maybe he should forget about football -- he's bound to blow it at tryouts. Thinking about tryouts is bumming him out. He goes home, flops on his bed and doesn't feel like doing anything..* • Do you ever dwell? What are examples of when you've dwelled?
Discussion: Awfulizing	Say: • Awfulizing is another type of negative thinking (also could be called Making a Mountain out of a Molehill or 'All or Nothing Thinking'). • Awfulizing happens when you take something that isn't such a big deal, but your thinking makes it a much bigger deal.

	• Here are some examples of Awfulizing thinking:
	  ○ "I got a bad grade... therefore, I'll never pass anything."
	  ○ "I struck out... therefore, I am the worst player ever."
	  ○ "I made a mistake... therefore, I never do anything right."
	  ○ "Jodi is mad at me... therefore, everyone hates me."
	• Do you ever make a big deal out of something that could stay little?

Activity: Stop Negative Thinking	• When you notice you are Dwelling or Awfulizing, you have the ability to stop the negative thinking and manage the stress it causes. • Remember, stress takes up your mental energy and negative thinking increases stress. • Using your Positive Thinking Journal might be one way to help stop the negative thinking and replace it with positive thinking. • There might be other ways to stop negative thinking. Let's brainstorm what someone could do (thoughts or actions) that could stop negative thinking and manage the stress. • Post on chart paper as students brainstorm (save the chart paper as the students may brainstorm effective stress management ideas):
Activity	Take a minute to add any new ideas to your Positive Thinking Journal.

LESSON 6

Session 6: What Matters to You	
Note: See Whole Classroom Lesson on Goal-Setting (Whole Classroom Lesson 5) Note to Group Facilitator on *Goal-Setting:* Two reasons that *Goal-Setting* is important: 1. A fundamental principle in a future-oriented society is that children should be well-oriented to future thinking. The ability to set and achieve goals (to plan ahead) is needed to manage stress within a future-oriented society. 2. As children become aware of stressors and able to manage stress, they are less likely to choose goal-defeating behaviors. Yet, viewing behaviors as goal-supporting/defeating requires the insight to connect *behavior* with the *achievement of goals*. Children skilled at setting short and long-term goals are able to view behaviors that hinder goal-achievement as *goal-defeating*. The motivation to select goal-supporting behaviors then increases and is internalized. Initially, students will do a poor or cursory job of goal-setting. The 'goal' for 'Setting Goals' is that students gradually improve ability to set achievable and reasonably challenging goals. This only happens when there is a long-term plan to support practicing goal-setting. It may help to use the term *"Begin with the End in Mind"* (From Covey: "7 Habits of Highly Effective People") rather than "Goal-Setting." *Begin with the end in mind* can precede activities throughout the school day, providing modeling and practice in planning and achieving goals. Long-term goals change over time. Children should get used to setting long-term goals even if, as observing adults, we may know them to be unrealistic, whimsical, and likely to change. As children grow in understanding of self and the world, goals will adjust. Goal-Setting begins with awareness of what matters to you (i.e., what you value; what is important to you). Knowing "What Matters" is the foundation for goal-setting or "beginning with the end in mind". <u>Below is an example of helping students to identify what matters to them (a foundation for goal-setting).</u>	
Instruction: What Matters to You?	Say: • When you know what matters to you, your motivation increases. • *Behavior* can be goal-*supporting* or goal-*defeating* depending upon whether the *behavior* gets you closer of further away from what matters to you. • It is important to be aware of behaviors that help you achieve what matters to you and the behaviors that put you further away from what matters to you. • If a person is stressed-out and doesn't manage the stress, he/she is more likely to engage in goal-defeating behaviors. • Achieving the things that matter to you puts you *much more in control of your life.*
Activity: "What Matters To Me" Checklist	Complete "WHAT MATTERS TO ME" checklist ("Values" and "What Matters" checklists found in Appendix): • Discuss things that matter to group members • Connect the importance of managing stress to achieving what matters to you. Collect, make copies (for future use) and return to students.

LESSONS 7 AND 8

	Sessions 7 and 8: Introduction to the "Challenge to Manage form		
	Note: It will at least 2 Sessions to Complete the Discussions about the Items on the Challenge to Manage form (find in Appendix and print for students).
Big Messages for these Sessions	1. The Challenge to Manage form or Stress Test is used as a tool to increase stress awareness.
	2. A Challenge to Manage form lists common reasons for stress, but not every reason for stress.
	3. A Challenge to Manage form can help a person to be more aware of their stress -- the first step in managing stress.
Discussion: Stress Awareness	*Say:*
	• In our first session together, we learned about stress and the 2 ways people react to stress.
	• Who can tell me the 2 ways people react to stress (a poster of the '2 Ways' should be visible and can be used to remind the group)? The two ways are:
	○ *Act/Behave* without thinking things through first (be impulsive)
	○ *Manage* the stress.
	• Today, we are going to work on the first step of *managing* stress.
	• The first step is stress *awareness: being aware of your stress* and knowing what your stressors (stress triggers) are.
	Show the Challenge to Manage form (SEE APPENDIX)
	• The Challenge to Manage form is a simple tool to improve stress awareness.
	Prompt Discussions (complete at least half of the Challenge to Manage form (Stress Test) items in the first session and the remainder in the second session):
	• *Remember to remind the group that stress uses up your mental or physical energy.*
	• Let's discuss each item on the Challenge to Manage form:
	• *"I have anxiety or worries" (too much thinking about something):* A check here means you have a lot of worries, anxiety or extra thinking going on in your mind:
	• Has anyone in the group had a day in which you would check this item? Discuss.
	• What goal-defeating behaviors may happen if you don't manage your worries?
	• *"I'm angry or frustrated about something (or angry at someone)"*: A check here means you are angry, mad, frustrated, annoyed, irritated about something or angry (etc.) at someone:
	• Has anyone in the group had a day in which you would check this item? Discuss.
	• What goal-defeating behaviors may happen if you don't manage your anger?
	• "*Feeling sad or low energy*": A check here means you are feeling bummed out or sad about something or you are tired, fatigued, or out-of-energy due to a stress in your life. Discuss.
	• Has anyone in the group had a day in which you would check this item? Discuss.
	• What goal-defeating behaviors may happen if you don't manage your sadness or low energy?
	• "*I have too much energy*": A check here means your energy level feels too high (you feel too hyper). This feeling is often caused by stress that you haven't stopped to think about and manage.
	• Has anyone in the group had a day in which you would check this item? Discuss.
	• What goal-defeating behaviors may happen if you don't manage your energy level?

	• *"School work challenges"*: A check here means that you are having a hard time managing something related to school work – you should also check if it's related to not understanding what you being asked to do, if homework wasn't done, is the class is too boring, or you are falling behind (or write in if there is another schoolwork reason):
	• Has anyone in the group had a day in which you would check this item?
	• What goal-defeating behaviors may happen if you don't manage schoolwork related stress?
	• *"Not getting my basic needs met"*: A check means that the person is feeling stress due to lacking nourishment (food), sleep, or feelings of safety:
	• Has anyone in the group had a day in which you would check this item?
	• What goal-defeating behaviors may happen if you don't manage stress related to basic needs?
	• *"I am doing negative thinking or negative self-talk"*: A check here means you are discounting the positive, mind-reading, or another type of negative thinking like dwelling or awfulizing:
	• Has anyone in the group had a day in which you would check this item?
	• What goal-defeating behaviors may happen if you don't manage negative thinking?
	• *"I carried something in today from home or my personal life"*: A check here means that you have something going on outside of school that is really on your mind – it may be something to do with family or friends):
	• Has anyone in the group had a day in which you would check this item?
	• What goal-defeating behaviors may happen you don't manage stress from home or personal life?
	• *"I have unfinished business I need to take care of and get off my mind"*: A check here means that you have things to care of that are on your mind.
	• Has anyone in the group had a day in which you would check this item?
	• What goal-defeating behaviors may happen if you don't manage your unfinished business?
	• *"I don't think there is anything going on right now that should keep me from getting back to work (just needed a quick break)"*: A check here means that you know you are having a hard time in school but you can't think of any specific problems or stress going on right now. You think maybe all you needed was a quick break to manage the stress:
	• Has anyone in the group had a day in which you would check this item?
Discussion: Challenge to Manage Form	*Say:* • The Challenge to Manage form (Stress Test) is an important tool to improve stress awareness. • It can help you to name (label) the type of stress you are experiencing that may be causing thoughts and feelings that can lead to goal-defeating behaviors. • *For this tool to work its magic, you have to use it.* • In our next 2 sessions we'll be learning new stress management strategies that you can use when you are aware of your stress. *Prompt Discussion:* • When and where should you use this tool (Challenge to Manage form/ Stress Test)? • Will it be OK with your teacher(s) if you took a minute during class to use a Challenge to Manage form when you feel stressed or when you notice goal-defeating behavior is starting?
Activity:	• Use the Challenge to Manage form (Stress Test) right now to assess your stress. Discuss results.

Important	*Notes to Facilitator:*
	• After the Challenge to Manage form (Stress Test) has been introduced and discussed, it is important that the tool is used.
	• *If appropriate, hand out laminated* Challenge to Manage forms as a 'gift' to group members.
	• Help group members find a secure and easily located place for them to keep it.
	Instruct:
	• Tell students that each session from now on will begin with sharing (discussion) about the group's use of the Challenge to Manage form (Stress Test) in between group sessions.
	• Each session will end with:
	    ○ Time to add ideas to your Positive Thinking Journal.
	    ○ Completing a Challenge to Manage form (Stress Test) (for practice).
	• Remind students to practice using the Challenge to Manage form in between sessions.

LESSON 9

	Session 9: Dealing with Stress:
	Stress Management Strategies (PART 1)
	NOTE: It is important that all who work with the students in the group understand that emphasis on using stress management strategies occurs after self-awareness and stress awareness have been explored. While other stress strategies are discussed earlier, the emphasis on stress strategies occurs near the end. It is left to the discretion of the group facilitators whether or not to introduce stress strategies earlier.
Big Messages for this Session	1. Being aware of your stress is an important first step.
	2. Being able to manage your stress well is the next step.
	3. Well-Managed stress leads to being better able to achieve what matters to you (goal-supporting)
	4. Poorly-Managed stress leads to goal-defeating behaviors.

Discussion	*Say:*
	• In the last two sessions we learned about the Challenge to Manage form and how to use it as a tool for stress awareness.
	• Being aware of your stress is important if you want to manage your stress well.
	• In the next two sessions we'll learn and practice strategies for managing stress.
	• Using stress management strategies will help you to be more in control of yourself and will usually lead to goal-supporting rather than goal-defeating behaviors.
	
	Prompt Discussion:
	• Before I begin teaching these strategies, I want to learn about what you already do (or have done in the past) to manage your stress.
	• Ask the group to share how they manage stress. Remind them (if the opportunity arises) that big feelings, avoidance, or acting impulsively are ways that people *react* to stress but aren't usually the best ways to *manage* stress.
	• If group members use examples like walking away or ignoring, tell them that these strategies *do work sometimes* (can be goal-supporting) but sometimes they don't solve the problem -- sometimes the stress continues and sometimes the stress gets bigger when things are avoided.
	• Ask the group to share what they've seen other people do to manage their stress.
	• How would you know if a stress management strategy worked?
	   ○ *Begin with the End in Mind.* If a stress management strategy (a "Stress Strategy") works, how would you be thinking, feeling, behaving?
	   ○ One answer for how you can tell if a strategy worked is that your thinking and feeling are settled enough to allow you to get back to goal-supporting behaviors.
	• How well do your current strategies work? How well do other people's strategies work?

Activity: Stress Management Strategy	*Say:* • It's time to learn and practice some new Stress Strategies. • The Stress Strategies we'll learn are not the only Stress Strategies – you've got to find strategies that work best for you. What we learn here may not turn out to be right for you. *STRESS STRATEGY:* Calming Breaths (Deep Breathing) Can be done standing, sitting or lying down. 1. Close your eyes. Put your hands on your stomach. 2. Keep your mouth closed and breathe in very slowly through your nose. Count to 6 in your head while you breathe in. Feel your stomach rise and expand while you breathe in. 3. Hold that air in your body while you count to 4 in your head. 4. Slowly let the air out through your mouth or nose. It should take about twice as long to release your breath as it took to breathe the air in. • Take 2 to 4 Calming breaths and then get back to your task. • Taking calming breaths can help make stress lighter and make you feel better at the moment. However, it may not eliminate the *source* of the stress. In addition to calming breaths you *may* need a plan to deal with the source of the stress (e.g., the person you are mad at). • Practice Calming breaths (deep breathing). Careful not to overdo it.
Discussion	*Ask:* • How did the breathing make you feel? • Did you feel silly doing it? • Can you picture yourself using calming breaths to reduce your stress? • How many of you think you might try calming breaths when you are aware of feeling stressed?
Instruct: Using Positive Thinking Journal as a Stress Management Strategy	*STRESS STRATEGY:* Positive Thinking Journal *Say:* • Positive thinking is hard to do when you're stressed out. • Negative thinking, like discounting the positive, mind-reading, awfulizing and dwelling are common types of thinking that everyone does. • Negative thinking can lead to goal-defeating behavior. • Positive thinking and positive self-talk can break a negative thinking cycle. • Using a Positive Thinking Journal is a strategy you can use to break a negative thinking cycle. • This is the process for using your Positive Thinking Journal as a stress management strategy: 1. First step is Stress Awareness – you need to be aware of the stress! 2. Use a Challenge to Manage form when you start to feel stressed or when behavior begins to be goal-defeating. Challenge to Manage form can also be used proactively when you aren't feeling stressed yet. It can help you think about what is happening in your life. 3. If you notice that you are doing negative thinking, *decide* to end the negative thinking cycle by implementing a positive thinking strategy. 4. Open your Positive Thinking Journal. 5. Find words, pictures, phrases, etc., that make you smile, laugh or inspire positive thinking. 6. Once your thinking has turned for the positive, your body should be feeling some stress relief. 7. You should be ready to get back to goal-supporting behavior! *Say:* • Positive thinking *may* help a lot. However, you may still need to plan to address the *source* of your stress.
Activity and Discussion	*Say:* • Everyone use a Challenge to Manage form (Stress Test) right now. Check off any items that are causing stress for you today. • After the Challenge to Manage form (Stress Test), use your Positive Thinking Journal (PTJ) to keep your thoughts positive. *Ask:* • Did anyone check off an item on the Challenge to Manage form? • Did anyone have negative thinking (negative self-talk) going on? • Even if you aren't having a lot of stress today, can your PTJ help you with positive thinking (positive attitude; improved mood)? • Can you picture yourself using your PTJ during school situations (i.e., during class)?

LESSON 10

	Session 10: Dealing with Stress: Stress Management Strategies (PART 2)		
Big Messages for these Sessions	• Being aware of your stress is an important first step. • Being able to manage (or deal with) your stress is the next step. • Well-Managed stress leads to goal-supporting behaviors (better able to achieve what matters). • Poorly-Managed stress leads to goal-defeating behaviors.		
Activity: Stress Test	*Say:* • Did anyone use a Challenge to Manage form (Stress Test) in between group sessions? o If so, please share the experience. • Everyone complete a Challenge to Manage form (Stress Test) now. • Check any items that are causing stress for you today. • If needed, implement a quick stress management strategy.		

Discussion	Say:
	• In the last session we discussed 2 strategies for managing or dealing with stress.
	  o Calming Breaths (Deep-Breathing).
	  o Positive Thinking Journal.
	• Today we'll talk about new strategies: Visual Imagery' Making a Plan, and making a list.
	• But first let's talk about whether you used the strategies we discussed last time.
	• If yes, talk about situation and tell us how it worked.
	• If no, why not?		

Introduce Visual Imagery	*Stress Management Strategy.* Visual Imagery
	• At first, this type of stress management strategy may seem a little strange.
	• However, these types of relaxation strategies actually can reduce stress so that a person can get back to goal-supporting behaviors.
	• They can work in a very short timeframe – within a few minutes.
	• There are 3 types of visual imagery that we'll learn today.
	  o 'Calm Place'
	  o 'Cast off the Chains'
	  o Visualize a successful outcome
	Note: See Whole Group Lesson 10 for full script for "Calm Place" and "Cast off the Chains".		

Activity: Calm Place	Imagery #1: Imagine a 'Calm Place' *Discuss:* • Why imagine a calm place?		

	○ This visualization can help a person to relax.
	○ It works best when the person is angry, frustrated, or anxious.
	Continue (See Whole Group Lesson 10 for full "Calm Place" script):
	• Calm Place is an easy visualization exercise.
	• All you need to do is close your eyes and think about a place where you are at ease.
	Activity:
	• Use 60 seconds of silence to think of a calm place.
	• Practice going to the calm place.
	• Discuss what it felt like to practice.
Activity: 'Cast off the Chains	Imagery #2: 'Cast off the Chains'
	Discuss:
	• Why imagine you are being freed from chains?
	○ Problems and stress can feel to a person like chains that are holding you down.
	○ Imagining being freed from chains gives a person the feeling of lightening the pressure.
	ACTIVITY (See Whole Group Lesson 10 for full "Cast off the Chains" script):
	Practice Cast off the chains.
	Discuss:
	Discuss what it felt like to practice this visual imagery strategy.
Activity: Visualize a Successful Outcome	Imagery #3: Visualize a Successful Outcome, or, Visualize "Begin with the End in Mind".
	• Studies have shown that athletes, actors and musicians who visualize successful outcomes in advance can increase their likelihood of success.
	• Therefore, many athletes imagine themselves hitting a successful shot in golf, hitting a baseball, or catching a football *before* they actually engage in the activity (THEY BEGIN WITH THE END IN MIND).
	• Actors visualize their performance and picture themselves receiving applause and praise (begin with the end in mind).
	• Musicians picture themselves playing their guitar or piano and singing successfully (begin with the end in mind).
	• Practice visualizing the following:
	1. Completing your homework successfully.
	2. Getting a good grade on a test.
	3. Having a positive conversation with someone you like but are nervous around.
	4. Having a successful experience in something that you do for a hobby or recreation.
	• Now plan to do the visualization right before you start the activity you are visualizing.
	• Using this strategy won't make all the things you want to happen come true, but it will provide positive thinking which will reduce stress, increase motivation, and make it more likely that you'll

	be successful.

Introduction: Make a Plan	Stress Management Strategy #4: Make a Plan
	• Often you will realize that your stress has to do with something unresolved or unfinished.
	• 'Unfinished business' is a good way to describe this type of stress.
	• With Unfinished Business, making a plan to finish it is a good stress management strategy.
	• An unresolved issue is something that is hanging over your head, you know you have to deal with it, but you'd rather not deal with it; you'd rather keep putting it off.
	• The unfinished business could be about:
	  o An argument, disagreement or conflict with a person in your life (friend, parent, sibling, teacher, peer).
	  o Getting behind in school work.
	  o A thank you card you are supposed to write to your grandmother.
	  o A bunch of things that need to get done.
	• A good plan helps relieve stress and leads to getting the 'business finished'.
	Handout a Planning Guide Template (see Appendix or Whole Group, Lesson 9) and Practice using the Planning Guide.

Instruct	• Another simple Stress Strategy is "Make a List". • This is a strategy to use when you have a bunch of things that need to get done. • Write them down and your stress will be reduced. • Then get them done to really relieve your stress!! • Use <u>Stress Strategies list</u> in the Appendix ("Address the Stress") for more ideas.

	Session 11: Closing Session
Big Messages	1. Group Closure 2. Review what was learned:. 3. Complete MS3 Survey (in Appendix)

Discussion	Say:
	• We've learned a lot of specific things (as items are stated, check for acknowledgement from group members and allow for brief discussion):
	• We learned about stress and what it means.
	• We learned the importance of being aware of what stresses you.
	• We learned that what stresses *you* may not stress me, and what stresses *me* may not stress you.
	• We learned how people deal with stress:
	• We learned that people react differently to stress:
	    ○ Some get mad, frustrated or angry; Some get bummed out or sad; Some get worried and anxious; Some get loud and annoying; Some get quiet, withdrawn and isolated;
	    ○ Some people try to ignore stress – they try to pretend that they have no stress.
	    ○ *Some people behave, or act, in whatever way they feel <u>without thinking things through</u> when they are stressed (act impulsively).*
	    ○ *Some people learn to be aware of their stress and learn how to <u>manage it</u> well.*
	• We learned the importance Beginning with the End in Mind and knowing what matters to you.
	• We learned that when your stress is well-managed, behavior is usually *goal-supporting* (you achieve the things that matter to you).
	• We learned that when your stress is not well-managed, behavior is often *goal-defeating* (you get further away from achieving things that matter to you).
	• We learned about some common reasons for stress like those on the Challenge to Manage form.
	• We learned how to use a Challenge to Manage form to help with the first step of Managing Stress: *<u>Stress Awareness</u>: Being Aware of Your Stress.*
	• We learned about "Self-Talk" and negative and positive thinking:
	    ○ We learned four specific kinds of negative thinking.
	• We learned positive thinking strategies (like a positive thinking journal), positive action strategies (like making a plan or a list), and other stress management strategies to help with the second step of Managing stress which is:
	    ○ *<u>Use a strategy to reduce or manage the stress.</u>*
	• We learned about the importance of *Persistence* and *Resilience (note: discuss this only if lessons for persistence and resilience were used – See Whole Classroom Lesson 6B: Persistence and Reilience).*
	• If you really use what we learned together, you will absolutely, positively be more successful:
	    ○ in school; in your friendships; in your relationships with family members; and eventually…. in your work when you are an adult
	• Let's talk for just a few more minutes about what you feel you learned and what you think you'll really use

(or have already used) as you move ahead with life. Discuss any further support or check-in that might help to sustain the learning once the group is officially over.

Take a moment to genuinely congratulate one another for the journey we took together in learning about stress and stress management. Thank the group for following the group norms for behavior and reflect briefly on what you learned (facilitator) as the leader of the group.

- Use an open discussion format or go around the group asking each member to speak -- *IF they are comfortable speaking.*
- When finished, ask students to complete the final survey (found in the appendix section).
- Adapt survey as needed to assess the fidelity of implementation and effectiveness of the group.
- Use a survey for teachers of students in the group to assess:
  - The teacher's use of strategies in the daily life of the student(s) in the group (if teachers were asked to use specific language, prompts, feedback, pre-corrects, or suggestions that emanated from group content).
  - Changes in student academic or social behavior since the start of the group.
  - Teacher assessment of the value of having the student attend this group.
  - What can be done to support teachers to help the students sustain learning?

Whole Class Lessons

(Written by E. Mann, Adapted by M. Lebrun)

LESSON 1: INTRODUCTION TO MANAGING STRESS

Lesson/Session 1—Desired Results

Established Goals:

1. Describe what *Managing Stress for School Success* program is all about.
2. Set group *Discussion Rules*
3. Complete *Managing Stress Survey*
4. The *Four Big Ideas About Stress*

Understandings:	**Essential Questions:**
1. Stress Awareness: being aware of the things that stress you and being aware of how stress affects you. 2. Stress Management: learning the skills to better manage stress so that stress doesn't stop you from achieving your goals or doing things that matter to you.	1. What is stress? 2. How do we identify stress and stressors? 3. How do we answer a survey honestly and correctly?

Students will be able to... will know....

1. Learn about what stress means.
2. Learn about stress awareness.
3. Learn ways to reduce and manage stress.
4. Participate in active listening and group discussions and brainstorms.
5. Become more aware of the things that stress you out (stress triggers)
6. Become more aware of how stress affects you and how you react to stress.
7. Learning the skills to better manage stress so that stress doesn't stop you from achieving your goals.
8. Become aware of the Four Big Ideas About Stress

Stage 2—Assessment Evidence

Performance Tasks:

1. Once or more a week the class will work on MS lessons.
2. Students will talk and learn about different types of stress, ways to manage and reduce stress through research and readings.
3. Students will use the internet and library to research different activities and information about stress.
4. Students will share about themselves in a completely voluntary, open and honest way.
5. Students are able to keep confidentiality within the classroom.
6. Students learn how to build trust with their classmates.

Stage 3—Learning Plan

Learning Activities:

1. Develop Ground Rules for Group Discussion:

Group Discussion Rules

We need to make some rules about having respectful discussions. Here are some common rules for having respectful discussions:

- One person talks at a time.
- Stay on topic.
- Stay positive with each other; avoid put-downs Do you have any other ideas?
- Write out your group discussion rules and post in the room to use as a reminder.

The Four Big Ideas About Stress (present to students as outline of future discussions)

#1: Everyone has stress.

#2: Things that stress you may not stress someone else…Things that stress someone else may not stress you.

#3: Stress can sometimes motivate people in positive ways.

#4: Stress sometimes leads to Frustration, Anger, Aggression, Big Worries, Sadness, or Giving Up

Lesson 1. Today, we'll discuss:

Idea #1: Everyone has stress!

Stressful things happen in life – to everyone! Anything that a person finds even a little bit annoying, difficult or challenging causes some stress.

Anything that requires any mental energy (thoughts) or physical energy causes stress. It may be useful to use a visual to demonstrate how stress uses mental or physical energy so that there isn't as much energy remaining to do your best academically or socially. Example: show an image of a brain with low stress – all areas able to function fully to complete work and social tasks. Then show a brain cluttered by stressful thoughts = less brain power is available for all your work and social time.

Some people say they are "stressed-out" when:

They feel overloaded or overwhelmed.

They have a lot to deal with or too much to get done.

They feel "pressure" or tension.

Something is bothering them.

When something is on their mind.

Discussion Prompts

Did you ever hear someone say they are "stressed out" (or did you ever say it)?

What do they (or you) mean? What causes stress for you?

Complete the **Managing Stress Survey** found in the Appendix.

Complete an analysis of the survey results and provide individual conferences with the teacher and student or have students work in small groups to discuss questions.

Additional adults can be incorporated to debrief results with group of students. The way the analysis will be done will depend on the characteristics and group dynamics of the individual classroom group.

It is imperative that the results be analyzed and shared to build self-awareness on the part of the student so that they can make the necessary correlations with the data and what their life experiences are.

Teacher will file the survey results for future collaborations with other teachers, parents, or administrators when working individually with the student.

Survey results can be aggregated to show profile of a specific grouping of students for future planning and strategy implementation when integrating certain models of behavior intervention or social skills training.

Next session we'll talk more about things that cause you stress.

Remind students of next meeting day and time.

LESSON 2: FOUR BIG IDEAS

Stage 1—Desired Results

Established Goals:

Discuss the *2ⁿᵈ Big Idea of Stress*. Help students become self-aware of what stresses them and why.

Understandings:	**Essential Questions:**

4 Big Ideas:
  1. Everyone has stress.
  2. Things that stress you may not stress someone else. Things that stress someone else may not stress you.
  3. Stress can sometimes motivate people in positive ways.
  4. Stress sometimes leads to Frustration, Aggression, Big Worries, Sadness, or Giving up.
	1. What situations or people stress you out?
	2. What situations or people don't stress you out?
	3. Why do some things, situations, or people bother other people and not you?

Students will be able to... will know...

1. Their stress triggers and what does not cause much stress (or make them stressed out) as compared to others in the class.
2. Will understand what triggers others in comparison to themselves.

Stage 2—Assessment Evidence

Performance Tasks:

1. Create a visible list of the group's stressors on chart Paper. (Make sure to keep for future reference)
2. Prompt till there are at least 10 stressors listed from the group

Stage 3—Learning Plan

Learning Activities:

    Discussion prompts:
    What stresses you out?
    Who can name something that bothers you, makes you feel mad, sad, frustrated, annoyed, embarrassed, or worried?
    Is there anything on the list that stresses someone else but doesn't bother you?
    Is there anything on the list that stresses you but doesn't bother other people?
    Explore solutions or techniques for managing stress.
    What works for you to calm down?

    Create a **Stress Journal**: students can draw or write about solutions for their stress (i.e. ways to manage their stress).

    Record individual stressors.

LESSON 3: BIG IDEAS STRESS 3&4

Stage 1—Desired Results

Established Goals:

1. Help students to integrate the idea that stress can be useful in helping an individual increase, build or develop motivation to do something new, challenging or exciting.
2. Increase student's awareness that when stress is not well managed it can lead to losing motivation to achieve things that matter to you.

Understandings:	Essential Questions:
Idea 3: Stress can sometime motivate people in positive ways Idea 4: Stress sometimes leads to Frustration, Anger, Aggression, Big Worries, Sadness, Giving up.	1. How is stress positive in your life? 2. How do you handle when you feel emotions about a situation or a person? 3. Can you think of a time when stress or pressure motivated you to achieve a goal or get something accomplished? 4. Can you think of a time when stress caused you to give up? Worry? Be angry and aggressive with someone?

Students will be able to... will know...

How to take negative or stressful specific examples and turn them into a positive experience. Students can become aware of their triggers and reactions when confronted with stressful situations.

Stage 2—Assessment Evidence

Performance Tasks:

Students will discuss in small groups a variety of case studies and identify the core emotions, thinking and responses to the case.
As a whole class solutions will be generated to deal effectively with the stress presented.
Students will identify how they can change their thinking and behaviors when next faced with a similar situation.

Stage 3—Learning Plan

Learning Activities:

Case Studies Scenarios: Present each case scenario for Big Idea 3. Discuss these examples (notice that in each example there is a pressure and tension, yet the person responds with positive actions and high focus). The goal will be to have students focus on the positive management of stress. You can also discuss what would happen if the individual did not manage the stress well, doing a compare and contrast chart might help students separate the reactions.

Big Idea 3
Situation 1: it's a tie game (baseball) it's up to me to get a hit; the pressure is on but my focus and determination are at the highest level.

Situation 2: I see my 3-year-old sister about to walk under a dangling tree branch; I get her out of the way quickly; I can't believe how fast I am.

Situation 3: have students come up with their personal experiences and debrief with them (formula: Stress = positive response and proactive thinking).

Big Idea 4

Discuss examples and notice how people in the example respond to pressure and tension (stress).

Situation 1: I have a lot of homework. I hate homework! I don't know why they have to give us homework every stinking night. I don't even know what I am supposed to do! The heck with it—I am done!

Situation 2: I am in a fight with my friend and I am going to see her on the bus this morning. I am SO mad at her that I completely spaced out and forgot to bring the money due today for the field trip. If anyone messes with me this morning they'll be sorry.

Situation 3: I bought a new shirt yesterday and I wore it today. A couple of kids made fun of it on the bus. I thought it was a cool shirt but I guess it's stupid. I'll never wear it again

Situation 4: Have students come up with their examples and process the thinking and redirecting it to a more positive reaction.

Journal entry: students can document and illustrate examples of positive stress reactions, and situations where they could have reacted differently.

LESSON 4: GOAL DEFEATING AND GOAL SUPPORTING BEHAVIOR

Stage 1—Desired Results

Established Goals:

1. Learn about *goal-defeating* and *goal-supporting* behavior.
2. Learn about different ways people behave under stress.

Understandings:	**Essential Questions:**
1. Reacting to stress (goal-defeating and goal-supporting behavior). 2. Behaviors that move you closer to your goals (closer to achieving something that matters to you) are called goal-supporting behaviors. 3. Behaviors that move you further from your goals are called goal-defeating behaviors. 4. Sometimes people ignore stress and try to pretend it isn't there. 5. Sometimes people react impulsively to stress. They behave without thinking. They do whatever they feel. 1. These responses to stress often lead to goal defeating behaviors. 6. It is important to know about yourself in order to understand the impact of stress. 7. Understanding who you are and knowing what matters to you (i.e. what you value) can help a person to understand why managing stress is important.	1. Do you ever ignore stress, or, behave without thinking? Act impulsively? 2. What are things you (behaviors, decisions, actions) do that are goal-supporting? Things you do that move you toward achieving your goals or values (the things that matter to you). 3. What are things you do (behaviors, decisions, actions) that are goal-defeating? Things you do that pull you away from achieving your goals or values. 4. What do people do and feel when they are stressed? 5. What types of feelings, behaviors or actions do you have when you experience stress?

Students will be able to... will know....

Goal-supporting behaviors vs. goal-defeating behaviors.

Goal-supporting behaviors are behaviors that keep a person on track to achieving his or her goals. Goal-supporting behaviors happen when a person is managing stress.

Examples: Practice guitar. Get your work done. Say something kind to a friend. Be on time for your job. Exercise.

Goal-defeating behaviors are behaviors that push a person further away from his or her goals (further from achieving things that matter to you). Goal-defeating behaviors happen when a person isn't dealing effectively with stress.

Examples: Give up on a task after one try. Disrupt class when you are unsure how to do the task (or if you are bored). Sleep all day when you've got things you know you have to do. Yell at your friend when you are really mad at someone else. Throw your project in the trash because you got frustrated.

Students will be able to name different responses to stress that are positive or negative responses.

Stage 2—Assessment Evidence

Performance Tasks:
The following inventories are used to guide discussions and increase self-awareness:

1. Values Assessment Survey ("What Matters"). See Appendix.
2. Self-Description Assessment. See Appendix.
3. Self- Assessment Data Summary Sheet. See Appendix.

Stage 3—Learning Plan

Learning Activities:

Please take out the self-assessment summary. Teachers please provide summaries to students who do not have theirs. Take a minute to look at what you said were your values, goals, dreams and bucket-list items.
Write down any new goals or insights that you've thought of since we did this activity.

Discussion Prompts:
What are things you (behaviors, decisions, actions) do that are goal-supporting?
Things you do that move you toward achieving things that matter to you (your goals or values).
What are things you do (behaviors, decisions, actions) that are goal-defeating?
Things you do that pull you away from achieving things that matter to you (your goals or values).

Students and Teachers To-Do:
During the next week try to be aware of things you do that help you to achieve things that matter to you (goal-supporting behaviors) and things you do that get in the way or harm your achievement of things that matter to you (goal-defeating behaviors). Share examples with each other throughout the week.

Teachers To-Do:
During the week, notice student behaviors that seem to be goal-supporting or goal-defeating.
Point out these behaviors when you see them.
Teachers use the goals/values and/or "What Matters" forms to summarize each student's goals and values. Make a copy for yourself and student.
Use the summaries to coach students and to strengthen your own knowledge about things that matter to students.

LESSON 5: SETTING GOALS

Stage 1—Desired Results

Established Goals:

1. Learn the importance of planning ahead.
2. Learn about three types of goals: *micro-goals*, *short-term goals,* and *long-term goals.*

Understandings:	Essential Questions:
There are two reasons that goal-setting is a feature in the Managing Stress for School Success curriculum: In a future-oriented culture or society, the ability to plan ahead is important (future thinking). The ability to set and achieve goals (plan ahead) is a foundation skill that is needed to successfully manage stress within a future-oriented society. It is important for children to learn the connection between their behavior and the achievement of goals. As children become more aware of their stressors and better able to manage stress, they will be less likely to engage in goal-defeating behaviors. But, in order for children to view behaviors as goal-defeating, they must be aware of their goals and aware of what matters to them. Only then are they able to gain the insight that behavior impacts the achievement of goals or the achievement of what you want. Once skilled at setting short and long-term goals, children can view behaviors that hinder goal achievement as goal-defeating behaviors -- not simply as behaviors that break the rules. The motivation, then, to choose behaviors that are goal-supporting is increased (and internalized). It is likely that students will initially do a poor or cursory job of goal-setting. The 'goal' for Setting Goals is that students gradually improve their ability to set achievable and reasonably challenging goals. It is also very likely that long-term goals will sometimes be whimsical and fantasy-driven. This should be expected and accepted. Long-term goals change over	**Ask and Discuss:** Are you the type of person who plans ahead or are you the type of person who takes things as they happen? Are you more or of a planner/goal-setter? Are you more of a spontaneous/impulsive person? **Discuss:** Do you think school is useful for your future? If you don't think so, can you think of something you do that *is* useful for your future?

time – even for adults. Children should get used to identifying long-term goals even if, as observing adults, we may know them to be unrealistic and likely to change. Adults should encourage future thinking even if it means accepting that some long-term goals are unlikely to be achieved. As children grow in their understanding of self and the world, their long-term goals will adjust.

Thinking about the future is easy for some people but difficult for others.
Setting goals pushes a person to think about the future. Some people don't like to plan ahead and prefer to deal with things as they happen.

Students will be able to... will know....

- School is a lot about the future.
- One of the goals of school is to prepare students for the future.
- If you are a spontaneous/impulsive person and not a planner/goal-setter then you probably don't plan ahead very much.
- Therefore, it might be hard for you to believe that school can be useful.
- If you really believed that school was helping you to achieve a goal for your future, then maybe school would seem more useful to you.
- Achieving goals that matter to you puts you in control of your life!

Stage 2—Assessment Evidence

Performance Tasks: Teach the concepts below and ensure students have an excellent understanding and mastery in the comprehension and differences before moving into the activities and evaluation summaries.

There are three types of goals:
1. Micro-goals
2. Short-term goals
3. Long-term goals

Micro-goals are usually planned in the moment. They are very short-term. They can be achieved within seconds and no longer than an hour.
Short-term goals are planned goals that will take longer than an hour from now to achieve but shorter than a month (note: there is really no cut-off, but we'll consider anything longer than a month ahead to be a long-term goal).
Long-term goals are planned goals that will take more than a month or even years to achieve.

Examples of micro-goals:
- Make 2 positive verbal comments by the end of this group session

- Stay awake and focused through the next 10 minutes of math class
- Record my homework assignment for social studies in my planner
- Smile and say hello to my English teacher when I see her at the start of next period
- Work hard and focused for the next 5 minutes

Examples of short-term goals:
- Complete ALL my homework by dinner time
- Be on time for school and class every day for the week
- Get all homework done this week
- Eat healthy every day (be specific about what you'll eat) for 3 weeks
- Argue with my brother fewer than 2 times per day for a month

Examples of long-term future goals:
- Make the basketball team next season
- Get a B or better in math
- Graduate high school
- Join the army
- Be a professional actor or singer
- Get a job in the construction business

Stage 3—Learning Plan

Learning Activities: Identification of the different types of goals. Teacher writes list on board or handout and asks students to identify what type of goal it is.

Activity (complete as a group):

Part 1: The following are examples of goals. For each one, please tell me whether you think it is a micro-goal, a short-term goal, or a long term goal.

___I really want to go to baseball practice today, so I have to get through each class with no behavior problems.

___My goal is to have perfect attendance in school for the next two weeks.

___It is September now and I am going to start running 2 miles a day so that when track starts in March I'll be ready.

___I am going to complete 4 math problems within the next 15 minutes.

___I want to be the first person in my family to go to college.

___I want to get through the next 30 seconds without blinking my eyes once.

___I am going to work to improve my free throw shooting from 50% this season to 60% next season.

Part 2: Look at your goals/values self-assessment summary from Lesson 4

Discuss:
Are the goals on your summary sheet mostly Short-Term Goals or Long-Term Goals?
Are there shorter goals (micro-goals or short-term goals) you could set that would help you to achieve a long-term goal?

Part 3: Practice setting goals

Use the Practice Goal Sheet (see below) and write:
1. A long-term goal.
2. A short-term goal that would help lead to your long-term goal.
3. A micro-goal that would help lead to your short-term goal.

Encourage students to make the goals *real*, goals that really matter to them.

Optional:
Use the Weekly Goal Sheet (see below) as a weekly goal-setting practice.
Allow time to for discussion/assessment of how the presence stressors impact the achievement of goals.
Promote the idea that when stress is light or well-managed, goal-supporting behavior is more likely.

Practice Goal Sheet

Name a **long-term goal**, something that you want to achieve that will take at least a couple of months, and could take many months or years to achieve. If this is difficult, try thinking about a long-term goal as a dream, a wish or a hope that you have (*Begin with the End in Mind*):

Name a **short-term goal** that will take longer than a day to achieve but you can achieve within a month that will help you to achieve your long-term:

Name a **micro-goal** that you can achieve right now within an hour that will lead you to achieve your short term goal:

Weekly Goal Sheet
For Weekly Goal-Setting and Goal-Assessment

What stressors did I have over the past week?

Did I achieve last week's goals? _____ Yes _____No

What is my goal (or goals) for next week?

LESSON 6A: SELF-TALK AND YOUR MOOD

Stage 1—Desired Results

Established Goals:

1. Learn about *self-talk*.
2. Learn about the impact of *negative thinking*.
3. Learn about the impact of *positive thinking*.
4. Start a *Positive Thinking Wall/Area* or *Positive Thinking Journal*.

Understandings:	Essential Questions:
Self-talk is something almost everyone does. Some self-talk is negative; we call this negative thinking. Negative thinking: Can bring you down; make you feel mad, sad or discouraged. Negative thinking can lead to goal-defeating behaviors. Negative thinking can be caused by stress and can add to stress Negative thinking can cause a bad mood. Here are examples of negative thinking: "This work is too hard" "That kid doesn't like me" "Everyone must be smarter than me" Some self-talk is positive; we call this positive thinking: Positive thinking can lift you up and make you feel hopeful and more confident. Positive thinking leads to goal-supporting behaviors. Positive thinking can reduce stress Positive thinking can cause a 'good mood'. Here are some examples of positive thoughts: "I can handle anything" "Even if I get something wrong or make a mistake it can't stop me"	***Discussion Prompts*** Are you: • An Optimistic/Positive thinker (hopeful, look on the bright side)? *OR* • A Pessimistic/Negative thinker (cynical, think the worst)? Even pessimistic thinkers can learn to think positively. What type of mood are you in right now? **"Good Mood" Examples:** Cheerful, Happy, Relaxed, Comfortable, Calm, Confident, Positive Energy… **"Bad Mood" Examples:** Irritated, Aggravated, Angry, Gloomy, Bummed Out, Sad Worried, Anxious, Uncomfortable Is anyone in the group in a "bad" mood right now? If so, let's talk about the stress you have going on. Can you name the stressors (i.e., stress triggers; things that cause you stress) you are dealing with today?

Students will be able to… will know…

Stress can lead to negative thinking.
Negative thinking is likely lead to a bad mood.
You can turn negative thinking into positive thinking and change your own mood.

Stage 2—Assessment Evidence

Performance Tasks: This session prompts the start of **Positive Thinking Wall** and/or a **Positive Thinking Journal**. Prepare for this activity in advance of the session.

- These positive thinking strategies are taught here in advance of other positive strategies that will be discussed in later lessons.
- *Since there is no single stress strategy that works for every person, the Positive Thinking Wall or Journal will not be an effective strategy for every student. Encourage students to try creating and using this strategy and analyze for themselves whether it works to help them stop negative thinking, improve their mood, and manage their stress.*

A strategy to help turn negative thinking into positive thinking (and improve your mood):
- Positive Thinking Wall
- Positive Thinking Journal

Stage 3—Learning Plan

Learning Activities: *Use positive thinking to stop negative thinking!*

- Start a Positive Thinking Wall/Area (group)
- Start a Positive Thinking Journal (individual)
- Start by brainstorming positive words, pictures, ideas, etc. that can go on the wall (or in the journal)

Create a visible Positive Thinking Wall or Area
Post written items, drawings, photos, etc. to the wall or area.

Ideas:
Post writings that could bring a smile to you or boost your energy.
Post events or dates that someone would look forward to.
Add photos or draw pictures of important things:
People who inspire you
Pets
Things that are fun for you
Post words that inspire positive thinking like "Confidence" or "Self-Control" or "Success" or "Persistence/Perseverance" "Resilience" or "Determination".
Post a favorite expression or quote that gives you a positive outlook or makes you laugh (examples):
"Embrace Life"
"If at first you don't succeed try, try again"
"To create more positive results in your life, replace "if only" with "next time.""
"It is only those who never do anything who never make mistakes."
"A positive attitude may not solve all your problems, but it will annoy enough people to make it worth the effort" (smile).

Positive Thinking Wall/Area
Use a wall in the room to create a Positive Thinking Wall/Area.
Use as a stress management strategy:
Look at it when negative thoughts are starting to affect your mood.
Use it to turn a negative mood into a positive mood by replacing negative thoughts with positive thoughts.

Positive Thinking Journal
Some students may want to create a Positive Thinking Journal for themselves—a booklet to develop yourself to inspire positive thinking.
Using a positive thinking journal is a "Stress Management Strategy."
Just like the positive thinking wall, fill it with positive ideas, pictures, drawings, expressions, words, inspirational quotes, etc.
You can look at it any time stress is building up or negative thinking is starting.
Or you can use it *proactively* to inspire a positive attitude!

LESSON 6B: PERSISTENCE AND RESILIENCE

Stage 1—Desired Results

Established Goals:

1. Learn what *persistence* means.
2. Learn what *resilience* means.

Understandings:	**Essential Questions:**
Persistence Persistence, or perseverance, is about the ability to refuse to give up, to be determined, to continue trying even when you are tired or frustrated. Being **persistent** means you have the ability to continue to try even in tough and difficult situations. Persistent people do not think about giving up; they think about how to solve the problem. Persistent people always find a way to get positive about the task they are attempting. Persistent people stay energized to complete the task. **Resilience** Resilience is about the ability to 'bounce back' or recover from a setback or a challenge. Being **resilient** means you have the ability to 'bounce back', rebound or recover from tough situations. Resilient people quickly think about how to re-start and get back to work even when something bad has happened. Resilient people always find a way to have a positive attitude. Resilient people always re-energize after a setback. Resilient people *get* right back on track when others might stay derailed.	Can you think of other examples of **persistence**? Please share and discuss. Have **you** ever been persistent? Can you think of other examples of **resilience**? Please share and discuss. Have **you** ever been resilient?

Students will be able to... will know....

The following are good times to think about persistence or resilience:
When you are aware that your behavior is off-track.
When you need to adjust your mood or attitude from negative to positive.

When you are aware of negative thinking.
When you are aware that you are stressed.
When you are tired or frustrated but you know you have a job to do.
When you are aware that your behavior is goal-defeating.

Persistence and Resilience
These are words that *every* successful person needs to know because being successful isn't easy.

Remembering these words when times are hard can remind you to stay positive and keep going

Stage 2—Assessment Evidence

Performance Tasks:

- Make sure "Persistence" and "Resilience" have space on the Positive Thinking wall after this lesson.

Let's make sure that the words "Persistence" and "Resilience" (and definitions) have space on our *Positive Thinking Wall.*

Persistence and resilience are not just important for school:
They are important for every part of your life.
They'll be important for your future life too.

Stage 3—Learning Plan

Research: Find a variety of historical, political, educational leaders and individuals who demonstrate or demonstrated persistence and resilience. Prepare a presentation.

LESSON 7: TYPES OF NEGATIVE THINKING

Stage 1—Desired Results

Established Goals:

Learn about different types of *Negative Thinking*:
- 'Discounting the Positive' (LSCI Institute, Senior Trainer Manual)
- Negative Mind-Reading (LSCI Institute, Senior Trainer Manual)
- Dwelling
- Making a Mountain out of a Molehill

Understandings:

Discounting the Positive
Discounting the Positive is a type of Negative Thinking. It happens when a person ignores everything positive about a situation and focuses only on the negative. What would you do if someone gave you a compliment?
For instance, if someone says:
"You drew an amazing picture."
"You have a nice smile."
"You have really good taste in clothes."
If you are discounting the positive, you may respond to a compliment by having negative *thoughts* like:
"You don't know me -- I'm terrible at drawing."
"My smile shows my big teeth and I look stupid."
Negative thoughts lead to negative feelings so you might respond to the compliment by saying "not really" or "I don't think so."
Or you might say "yeah, right" or roll your eyes and say "whatever."

Dwelling
Do you ever lie on your bed, sit on the couch, or sit at your desk and just think over and over about something?
It might be something you said or something you did that keeps replaying in your mind.
It might be something that you are worried about.
It might be about something you are dreading or not looking forward to.
It might be about something someone else said (or did) that makes you angry, worried, or bummed out.

Making a Mountain out of a Molehill
When you *Make a Mountain out of a Molehill* (also known as 'Awful-izing' or 'All or Nothing Thinking'):
"I got a bad grade... therefore, I'll never pass anything."
"I struck out... therefore, I am the worst player ever."
"I made a mistake... therefore, I never do anything right."
"Jodi is mad at me... therefore, everyone hates me."

Negative Mind Reading
Negative mind-reading is a type of negative thinking that almost everyone does.
Important points to remember about Mind-Reading:
When you Mind-Read, sometimes you are right, BUT sometimes you are wrong.
When you Mind-Read you might jump to the wrong conclusions

Essential Questions:

What negative thoughts would *discount the positive* and turn your mood/feelings downward?
What *positive thoughts* might keep your mood positive?
Do you ever discount the positive?
Do you ever think you know what someone else is thinking?
Do you ever think that someone is thinking something bad about you?
Do you ever predict in your mind that someone will be unfair, unhelpful or unkind?
Do you ever *dwell*?
Do you ever make a big deal out of something little?

Stage 2—Assessment Evidence

Performance Tasks:

Group Leader: *This session may take longer than one session to complete (depending upon discussion time and use of additional examples).*

Negative Mind Reading
Examples:
"I didn't ask Melanie to go to the mall with me because I knew she'd say 'no.'"
"I didn't tell the coach that the kid was giving me a hard time because I knew he wouldn't do anything about it."
"I never go to the after school club because all the kids in that club hate me."
"When I walked into my classroom today everyone was thinking that my new hair looks stupid".
Notice I didn't say these statements are never true—they *could* be true—but when we mind-read, we jump to conclusions. And when we mind-read, sometimes we jump to the **wrong** conclusions since we don't have all the information to know for sure.

Stage 3—Learning Plan

Learning Activities:

1. Brainstorm examples of each type of negative thinking, you can use the existing examples as springboard for discussion.
2. Draw a chart with all 4 types of Negative thinking.
3. Students can keep track of the statements made that are found within the categories, tabulate the results, do a graph, and set goals for decreasing the amount of negative thinking phrases individually, small groups or whole class. This can be integrated as a math lesson as well.

Catch Them Being Positive game, each time someone can reframe a negative statement for another student in a positive way, they can do a check or a point or put in a ticket in a jar for a daily drawing or recognition at the end of the day as a way to enhance positive reinforcement.

LESSON 8: STRESS AWARENESS AND STRESS TESTS

Stage 1—Desired Results

Established Goals:

1. Be aware of what stresses you (and what is triggering your stress) and how stress impacts you.
2. Use a *stress reduction* or *stress management strategy*.
3. Learn about the *Stress Test form* (also known as "The Challenge to Manage" form)
4. Learn the value of using the *stress test* form to improve *stress awareness*.

Understandings:	Essential Questions:
1. Sometimes people try to ignore stress; try to pretend it isn't there. 2. When people feel stress, they just act (or behave without thinking. 3. There are many ways a person reacts to stress. 4. The best way to get goal supporting results is to deal with your stress; learn to manage it or reduce it. 5. It is important to take control of your stress before it takes control of you.	1. How do you react to stress? 2. Do you know what stresses you out? 3. How do you know if stressors are present right now? 4. Do you know how you react to stress?

Students will be able to... will know....

1. Be aware of their own stress
2. Use strategies to reduce or manage stress

Stage 2—Assessment Evidence

Performance Tasks:

1. In previous discussions in earlier lessons, students discussed their feelings and what stressed them out (stress triggers). Students have also discussed the different ways people show stress in their behaviors. Review chart or list from previous discussion before beginning.
2. Introduce the Stress Test, explain purpose, it is a simple tool to help improve stress awareness. Using the stress test helps students become more aware of how their current stress may be impacting them.
3. Briefly review the form together before beginning.
4. Do Stress Test ("Challenge to Manage": found in Appendices)
5. Discuss and process student answers. This can be done in large group, small groups or individually depending on the students.
6. Discuss each one of the items individually with the group. Have students identify if any of the categories create stress for them.
7. Possible questions for each item on the stress test:

Item 1: Has anyone had a day in which you could check this item? What goal-defeating behaviors could happen if you don't reduce or manage the worries, anxiety or the extra thinking that is going on in your mind?

Item 2: Has anyone in the group had a day in which you could check this item? What goal-defeating behaviors may happen if you don't reduce or manage your frustration or anger?

Item 3: Has anyone in the group had a day in which you could check this item? What goal-defeating behaviors may happen if the person doesn't manage your sadness or low energy level?

Item 4: Has anyone in the group had a day in which you could check this item? What goal-defeating behaviors may happen if you don't manage your energy level if it's too high?

Item 5: Has anyone in the group had a day in which you could check this item? What goal-defeating behaviors may happen if you don't manage your school-work challenges?

Item 6: Has anyone in the group had a day in which you could check this item? What goal-defeating behaviors may happen if you don't manage the stress that come from not getting basic needs met?

Item 7: Has anyone in the group had a day in which you could check this item? What goal defeating behaviors may happen if you don't manage your negative thinking?

Item 8: Has anyone in the group had a day in which you could check this item? What goal-defeating behaviors may happen if you don't manage the stress and deal with the home or personal issue?

Item 9: Has anyone in the group had a day in which you could check this item? What goal-defeating behaviors may happen if you don't figure out a plan to get the unfinished business done or at least temporarily off your mind?

Stage 3—Learning Plan

Learning Activities:

1. Large group discussions can be incorporated as class meetings, responsive classroom activities, journal reflections and individual reflection.
2. For younger children they can illustrate some of their responses.
3. For upper elementary, middle and high school students these responses can be correlated with literature, characters or role models.

LESSON 9: STRESS MANAGEMENT PART 1

Stage 1—Desired Results

Established Goals:

1. Learn that there are many effective ways to deal with stress.
2. Think about what stress strategy works for you.
3. Practice *Deep Breathing exercises.*
4. Review the *Managing Stress Planning Guide.*

Understandings:	Essential Questions:
Stress Management Strategies can help you to: • Reduce the feeling of stress • Feel calmer • Feel more in control of yourself • Decrease negative thinking • Decrease negative feelings • Improve your mood • Continue (or resume) goal-supporting behavior • Resolve or address important issues that are bothering you • Leave behind (let go of) things that are less important • Leave behind (let go of) things you have little control over	1. How does one deal with stress? 2. What stress strategies work best for you? 3. What is deep breathing and how do I use it to calm myself down? 4. How can I use the stress planning guide effectively to help me with my stress?

Students will be able to... will know....

Make a Plan to Manage the Stress:
Sometimes using a positive thinking strategy or a positive action strategy will help reduce your stress and you'll be able to continue goal-supporting behaviors.
But, sometimes you'll really need to make a plan to deal with the source of your stress.

Unfinished Business
Very often stress has to do with something that is unresolved or unfinished.
An unresolved issue is something that is hanging over your head -- you know you have to deal with it but maybe you'd rather not deal with it.
Maybe it feels easier to keep putting it off or avoiding it.
"Unfinished Business" is a good way to describe this type of stress.

Stage 2—Assessment Evidence

Performance Tasks:

Activity: Dealing Effectively with Stress
Take a few minutes individually to carefully look at what stresses you out.

Group Leader:
Decide if and how to practice using the Planning Guide with your students.
Once students are comfortable using the form, its use can be suggested when a student is showing signs of stress or is engaging in goal-defeating behavior.

Stage 3—Learning Plan

Learning Activities:

Note:

- The Stress Reduction and Stress Management strategies in the next 2 lessons should represent the beginning of an exploration of effective strategies.
- Each student will need to find strategies that work for him/her and all will respond differently to the ideas presented here.
- There is no strategy that works for everyone.
- All strategies must be practiced repeatedly to have a realistic chance of being learned and applied at the right times.
- It is recommended that the work begun using Managing Stress for School Success be reviewed and expanded upon using:
    - Other topically related curricula (Cognitive Behavioral Treatment; Mindfulness; Emotional Regulation Skills curricula; Executive Skills curricula)
    - Literature: Both fiction and non-fiction provide endless examples of people experiencing stress, reacting to stress, managing stress effectively and managing stress poorly. Use examples in literature to point out goal-defeating and goal-supporting behaviors, connecting management of stressors to thoughts, feelings, behaviors and outcomes.
    - Current events also provide countless examples of stress and stress management.
    - Please use all of the above concurrently with the curriculum as possible, and after the lessons are complete.

Stress Management Strategy:
Calming Breaths (Deep Breathing)
This can be done standing, sitting or lying down.
Review the instructions completely once before practicing the breathing strategy.

1. Close your eyes. Put your hands on your stomach.
2. Keep your mouth closed and breathe in very slowly through your nose. Count to 6 in your head while you breathe in. Feel your stomach rise and expand while you breathe in.
3. *Hold that air in your body* while you count to 4 in your head.
4. Slowly let the air out through your mouth or nose.
5. Repeat 2 to 4 times.
6. Then get back to your goal-supporting behavior!

Depending on the readiness of your students to use the Planning Guide below it is recommended that you use it as a follow up tool for helping individual students and possibly small groups.

Deal with the Stress: Planning Guide

First Step: Decide what I need to do:
- ☐ Make a plan to get caught up on my school work:
  (who can help me get caught up)?_____).
- ☐ Talk to the person I am mad at:
  (who is it?_____).
- ☐ Arrange time to talk to a trusted person about the problem or issue:
  (who will I talk to ?_____).
- ☐ Take care of unfinished business:
  What is the unfinished business?_____.

Next Step: Find the time:
Decide when you are going to take the next step to solve the problem (i.e., do what you checked above).
- ☐ Today at _____ (Time)
- ☐ Tomorrow at _____(Time)
- ☐ Other _____(Day and Time)

Next Step: Describe exactly what I am going to do:
- ☐ Talk to _____ about helping me make a plan to get caught up on my work.
- ☐ Talk to _____ to work out our disagreement.
- ☐ Talk to (or set up a time to talk to) _____ about something I need some help with.
- ☐ Take care of my unfinished business by doing the following:
  _____
  _____

LESSON 10: STRESS MANAGEMENT PART 2 AND CLOSURE

Stage 1—Desired Results

Established Goals:

Learn and practice *Visual Imagery strategies*:
- Visualize a Positive Outcome
- Calm Place
- Cut off Chains

Understandings:	Essential Questions:
There are several strategies that can help calm and take you to a place of reflection and quiet.	1. How does visual imagery work? 2. How can I get to a place of calm? 3. How I can silence my brain and be quiet?

Students will be able to... will know....

Visual Imagery strategies are relaxation or positive thinking strategies that will work for **some** people to help reduce and manage stress.

Some people will like these and some won't.

Remember, just as stress is different for everyone, what works for you to manage it will be unique too.

Visual Imagery : Visualize a Successful Outcome

Plan to do the visualization right before you actually start the activity you are visualizing.

Using this strategy won't make all the things you want to happen come true, but it will produce positive thinking which will:

Reduce your stress.

Increase your motivation.

Make it more likely that you'll be successful at the task.

Stage 2—Assessment Evidence

Performance Tasks:

Visual Imagery: Visualize a Successful Outcome

Studies have shown that athletes, actors and musicians who visualize successful outcomes in advance of their performances can increase their likelihood of success.

Many athletes actually imagine themselves hitting a successful shot in golf, hitting a baseball, or catching a football **before** they actually engage in the activity.

Actors visualize their performance. They picture themselves acting, and then receiving applause and praise.

Musicians picture themselves playing their guitar or piano and singing successfully.

The power of positive thinking reduces stress or channels your stress into goal-supporting behavior.

Visual Imagery: Cast off the Chains

Problems and stress can feel like chains that are holding you down.

In this visual imagery strategy, you'll imagine yourself as you are freed from these chains.

Imagining this can give a person the feeling of lightening the pressure.

This strategy can allow a person to feel a reduction in stress as the 'chains' are released.

It can help a person keep in perspective things that matter and things that you need to let go of.

It can remind a person to focus on what they can control and to release what they can't control.

Reducing the pressure of the chains of stress can put a person in control of their lives and keep them on-track to goal-supporting behaviors

Food for Thought

Learn Mindfulness, Meditation, Yoga or Body Relaxation:

Learn to clear your thoughts and your stress.

Learn to relax and calm down.

Learn to focus on being 'in the present': Be aware of your present thoughts, feelings and body sensations.

Learn what you can control in the future without worrying about the past.

The strategies named above take some time to learn:

Your group may consider making a plan to learn more about one or more of these strategies.

Manage IT!

Stress Awareness:

- ❏ Name your feelings
- ❏ Name your stressors

❑ Use a Stress Test Form
❑ Identify your negative self-talk or negative thinking

Stress Reduction and Stress Management Strategies:

❑ Take two or three deep Calming Breaths (Deep, Slow Breathing)
❑ Try a visual imagery relaxation strategy ('Calm Place'; 'Visualize a Successful Outcome'; 'Cast off the Chains')
❑ Take a brief exercise or movement break (safe, but physical)
❑ Draw a ZenTangle (see www.zentagle.com)
❑ Use positive self-talk or positive thinking
    ❑ Look at your positive thinking journal
    ❑ Look at the Positive Thoughts Wall (area)
    ❑ Read something positive, inspirational, or funny
    ❑ Call your 'Positive Thinking Partner'
❑ Write about your stress and feelings
❑ Draw about your stress and feelings
❑ Talk about your stress and feelings to a trusted person (friend, teacher, counselor, parent)
❑ Resolve or deal with the person you are frustrated with, angry with, or concerned about
❑ Make a plan:
    ❑ Take care of unfinished business (make a plan to handle the issue that is on your mind)
    ❑ Set an achievable goal and make a step by step plan to achieve it
    ❑ Make an organizational plan to get caught up on your work

---

Stage 3—Learning Plan

Learning Activities:

Visual Imagery : Visualize a Successful Outcome

Close your eyes and visualizing each the following:

Visualize getting a good grade on a test.

Picture getting your homework done.

Imagine having a positive, calm conversation with someone you like but are nervous around.

See yourself having a successful experience with something that you do for a hobby or fun:
- Skiing
- Sinking a basket
- Running a race
- Cooking and presenting a delicious meal
- Playing your musical instrument

Visual Imagery: "Calm Place"

Visualizing a *Calm Place* can help a person to relax and reduce stress.
It can work for a person who is feeling angry, frustrated, anxious, or bummed out.

To use this strategy, all you need to do is close your eyes and think of a place where you are at ease.

In other words, think of a place where you feel calm, safe, relaxed and comfortable.

Many people visualize the beach, a mountaintop, or on a lake fishing or rowing.

Your 'place' could be where there are peaceful sounds: waves; music; nature.

It may be where you feel warmth of the sun or a cool breeze.

It may be a place where you see the stars or a sunset.

It may be a place where you have fun.

Your place could be somewhere you've never been to, or a place you go to all the time.

It could be completely imaginary, make believe, or magical.

It is important to use all your senses: Think about what you see, hear, smell and feel when you are at this safe and calm place.

Wherever and whatever that place is -- it's up to you! No one can stop you from going to the calm place in your mind.

Activity:

Allow 30 seconds for students to think of their 'Calm Place.'

Then provide 60 seconds of silence for thinking.

As they are thinking, gently remind them to use all senses -- think about what you see, hear, smell and feel when you are at your safe and calm place.

Discuss what it felt like to use this strategy.

Visual Imagery: "Cast off the Chains" (Optional, if time allows and group is responsive to visual imagery)

1. Close your eyes.
2. Imagine that you are wrapped in heavy chains.
3. Feel the chains pulling you down.
4. You can barely move at all.
5. You are stuck; you are unable to move at all in the chains.
6. Now slowly, gradually....you start to feel the chains loosen up.

7. In your mind, you can see and feel the chains loosening and hear them clattering to the ground around your feet.
8. You are finally free from the chains!
9. Now (in your mind) pick them up and throw them away.
10. Feel how light you are; take that feeling with you as you step back into your day.
11. You are ready to take control of your day.

Discuss: Discuss what it felt like to practice this visual imagery strategy.

Group Leader:

- Remind the Group that the next session will be the final session for the group.
- Address concerns for sustaining ongoing connections to the group and the leader.
- Allay concerns or validate feelings but sustaining your (group leader's) connection with students.
- If group is able to re-convene, discuss what the goals would be and address practical considerations (if reconvening the group is a viable/desirable option).

CLOSURE – FINAL SESSION ON STRESS MANAGEMENT

Established Goals:

1. Summarize what was learned.
2. Complete surveys.

Group Leader:

We've learned a lot of specific things (as items are stated, check for acknowledgement from group members):

- We learned about stress.
- We learned that everyone deals with stress.
- We learned about the importance of being aware of what stresses you.
- We learned that what stresses *you* may not stress me, and what stresses *me* may not stress you.
- We learned that people react differently to stress:
- Some people get mad, frustrated or angry.
- Some people get bummed out or sad.
- Some people get worried and anxious.
- Some get loud and annoying; others get quiet and isolated.
- Some people try to ignore stress – they try to pretend that they have no stress.
- Some people behave, or act, in whatever way they feel without thinking things through (when they are stressed).
- Some people learn to be aware of their stress and learn how to deal with it, manage it, reduce it or 'let it go.'
- We learned the importance of having goals.

- We learned that when your stress is well-managed, behavior is usually **goal-supporting**.
- We learned that when your stress is not well-managed, behavior is often **goal-defeating**.
- We learned about common reasons for stress.
- We learned how to use a Stress Test (Think about It Sheet) to help with the first step of Managing Stress: **Stress Awareness: Being Aware of Our Stress**.
- We learned a number of positive thinking strategies, positive action strategies and stress management strategies to help with the second step of Managing stress: **Use a strategy to reduce or manage the stress.**
- We learned about the importance of **Persistence** and **Resilience.**
- If you really use what we learned in our work together, you will absolutely, positively be more successful:
  - in school
  - in your friendships
  - in your relationships with family members
  - and eventually, in your work when you are an adult

- Let's talk for just a few more minutes about what you feel you learned and what you think you'll really use (or have already used) as you move ahead with life.

Use an open discussion format or go around the group asking each member to speak **IF they are comfortable speaking.**

When finished with the discussion, ask students to complete the final surveys found in the appendix section.

Conclusion

The journey of stress awareness and stress management is far from over. As long as there are human beings, situations, relationships, environmental factors and disasters, and people have the ability to think, stress will be an important component of our lives. Stress is often portrayed as a negative coping mechanism but often it is the catalyst for change and growth. Without having healthy stress we have the possibility of being stagnant. Advancement and innovation will be part of the legacy of the past and not instrumental in development of new ideas and new frontiers.

Poorly managed stress and anxiety is alive and well, it is evident in the heart attack and stroke statistics we see in the media. People are often aware of the stress, they feel it every moment of the day, yet do little to regulate it. They continue impulsive behaviors till their body or minds can no longer sustain a healthy existence. Societal expectations have moved at alarming rate of speed. Many children, adolescents, and adults cannot maintain the level of mental or physical energy required to be successful or even keep up. The end result is that they check out. In some instances physical and mental health issues, substance misue, and early death are the outcomes.

This book's focus has been on how to educate children, adolescents, and the adults who were with them to become better advocates for themselves when it comes to stress management. Building stress knowledge and awareness at an early age empowers these children and adolescents to be better equipped at dealing with stress as adults. Teaching the skills at school where stress management becomes part of the educational experience helps cement the knowledge for years to come. Students learning effective coping and management skills while they are in a safe and nurturing environment enables them to generalize some of the skills to life outside of school.

In conclusion, this book has been a journey of exploration, reflection, and application.

Appendix A

Managing Stress for School Success

SURVEY

1. **What makes you feel stressed (or feel "stressed out")?**

CIRCLE YOUR LEVEL OF AGREEMENT FOR EACH STATEMENT:

2. **Stress causes some people to get mad or frustrated.**
   1 = Strongly Agree   2 = Agree   3 = Not Sure   4 = Disagree   5 = Strongly Disagree

3. **Stress causes some people to give up or quit.**
   1 = Strongly Agree   2 = Agree   3 = Not Sure   4 = Disagree   5 = Strongly Disagree

4. **Stress causes some people to be physically aggressive.**
   1 = Strongly Agree   2 = Agree   3 = Not Sure   4 = Disagree   5 = Strongly Disagree

5. **Some people don't experience stress at all.**
   1 = Strongly Agree   2 = Agree   3 = Not Sure   4 = Disagree   5 = Strongly Disagree

6. **Stress causes some people to get nervous or worried.**
   1 = Strongly Agree   2 = Agree   3 = Not Sure   4 = Disagree   5 = Strongly Disagree

7. **Things that stress one person might not stress someone else.**
   1 = Strongly Agree   2 = Agree   3 = Not Sure   4 = Disagree   5 = Strongly Disagree

8. **All people react the same way when they are stressed.**
   1 = Strongly Agree   2 = Agree   3 = Not Sure   4 = Disagree   5 = Strongly Disagree

9. **Sometimes people like to ignore stress or pretend not to have stress even when they feel stress.**
   1 = Strongly Agree   2 = Agree   3 = Not Sure   4 = Disagree   5 = Strongly Disagree

10. **Negative thinking can lead a person into a bad mood.**
    1 = Strongly Agree   2 = Agree   3 = Not Sure   4 = Disagree   5 = Strongly Disagree

11. **A person can change their mood by using their thoughts.**
    1 = Strongly Agree   2 = Agree   3 = Not Sure   4 = Disagree   5 = Strongly Disagree

12. **Slow, deep breathing can reduce stress for some people.**
    1 = Strongly Agree   2 = Agree   3 = Not Sure   4 = Disagree   5 = Strongly Disagree

13. **Being hungry or tired can cause stress.**
    1 = Strongly Agree   2 = Agree   3 = Not Sure   4 = Disagree   5 = Strongly Disagree

CIRCLE THE BEST ANSWER

14. **Goals can be:**
    a. Long term (far from now)
    b. Short term (days, or even minutes, from now)
    c. Either long term or short term
    d. Not sure

15. **Making a plan to resolve something that's been on your mind is likely to:**
    a. Add stress
    b. Reduce stress
    c. Not sure

16. **What is the definition of *Persistence*?**
    a. Continuing to try even when things are difficult
    b. A really bad cough
    c. Always doing the opposite of what someone asks
    d. Not sure

17. **What is the definition of *Resilience*?**
    a. Refusal to accept what someone is telling you
    b. The ability to bounce back, rebound, or recover
    c. A feeling of great power
    d. Not sure

18. **What are you doing if you are "dwelling"?**
    a. Drawing
    b. Getting stuck on a thought
    c. Getting organized
    d. Spending money
    e. Not sure

19. **What are strategies that you use to *manage stress* or *reduce stress*?**

Appendix B

CHALLENGE TO MANAGE FORM ("STRESS TEST")

	The *Challenge to Manage*
	Date: _____ Student Name: _____ Time of Day: _____
☐	"I have anxiety or worries" (too much thinking about something)
☐	"I am angry or frustrated about something (or angry at someone)"
☐	"Feeling sad or low energy"
☐	"I have too much energy"
☐	"School work Challenges": ☐ I don't understand what I am supposed to do ☐ My homework wasn't done ☐ Class is too boring ☐ I'm falling behind in my work
☐	"Not getting my basic needs met": ☐ Not enough food ☐ Not enough sleep ☐ Feeling unsafe
☐	"I am doing negative thinking or negative self-talk": ☐ Dwelling ☐ Mind Reading ☐ Discounting the Positive ☐ Awfulizing – Making a mountain out of a molehill
☐	"I carried something in today from home or my personal life".
☐	"I have unfinished business I need to take care of and get off my mind".
☐	"I don't think there is anything going on right now that should keep me from getting back (just needed a quick break)".

Source: Mann, 2015.

STRESS TEST

If you checked:	Think about it:
"I HAVE EXTRA WORRIES, SADNESS OR STRESS TODAY."	"What is worrying me? What is making me feel stressed or summed out? How can I deal with this so it doesn't mess up my day?"
"I'M ANGRY OR FRUSTRATED ABOUT SOMETHING (OR ANGRY AT SOMEONE)."	What am I angry or frustrated about? Who am I angry with? How can I avoid taking out my anger where it doesn't belong? How can I deal with it so that I don't make things worse for myself?
"DOING SCHOOL WORK IS FRUSTRATING." ☐ I DON'T UNDERSTAND WHAT I AM SUPPOSED TO DO ☐ MY HOMEWORK WASN'T DONE ☐ IT'S TOO BORING ☐ I AM NOT FEELING SAFE	Can I be persistent or resilient? How can I deal with the stress without getting myself into goal-defeating behavior like: ☐ Giving up ☐ Refusing to work ☐ Avoiding
"I AM NOT GETTING MY BASIC NEEDS MET": ☐ I DIDN'T GET ENOUGH SLEEP LAST NIGHT (LATELY) ☐ I DIDN'T EAT BREAKFAST ☐ I AM NOT FEELING SAFE	Who can I talk to about this?
"MY ENERGY LEVEL IS: ☐ TOO HIGH ☐ TOO LOW"	I need to slow myself down or get myself energized for school so that I avoid goal-defeating behavior
"I AM DOING NEGATIVE THINKING OR NEGATIVE SELF-TALK": ☐ DWELLING ☐ MIND READING ☐ DISCOUNTING THE POSITIVE ☐ AWFULIZING – MAKING A MOUNTAIN OUT OF A MOLEHILL	I'm aware of negative thinking, so now I need to think about something positive. Look at my Positive Thinking Journal for ideas.
"I CARRIED SOMETHING IN TODAY FROM HOME OR MY PERSONAL LIFE"	I need to deal with what is going on so that I don't take my frustrations out on others or give up on my school work.
"I HAVE UNFINISHED BUSINESS I NEED TO TAKE CARE OF AND GET OFF MY MIND"	I need to make a plan to get caught up on my work, or make the call I've been putting off, or get that present for my mother, or...
"I DON'T THINK THERE IS ANYTHING GOING ON RIGHT NOW THAT SHOULD KEEP ME FROM DOING MY WORK"	Maybe I just need a quick break or a deep breath to get myself back on track,

Appendix C

Goals, Values, and Bucket List

Self-Assessment: *Goals, Dreams and 'Bucket List'*	
(a "Bucket List' item is something you want to do someday)	
Put a checkmark to the left of each item below that is a Goal, a Dream, or a 'Bucket List' item for you:	*Put a checkmark to the left of each item below that is a Goal, a Dream, or a 'Bucket List' item for you:*
☐ Get Better Grades	☐ Worry Less
☐ Break a Record (if you have a specific record you want to break, write it here: _____)	☐ Be a Leader
☐ Graduate High School	☐ Have Peace of Mind
☐ Go to College or Graduate College	☐ Go to Outer Space
☐ Eat Healthier	☐ Join the Military
☐ Own a Car	☐ Get Married
☐ Exercise More	☐ Be a Father or a Mother
☐ Increase My Reading Speed	☐ Run (complete) a Long Race (like a marathon or triathlon)
☐ Have Better Control of My Emotions	☐ Drive a Race Car
☐ Work as a Volunteer to Help People	☐ Own a House
☐ Travel the World	☐ Have a lot of Money (Be Rich; Be Wealthy)
☐ Get a Paying Job	☐ Be a Professional Musician (A Singer, Guitar Player, Piano Player, Drummer, etc.)
☐ Have Nicer Clothes	☐ Play an instrument as a Hobby
☐ Skydive	☐ Have a Role in a Movie or TV Show
☐ Get Tutored in _____	☐ Live Independently (not with parents)
☐ Be More Easy Going	☐ Be a _____ (name a job or occupation if you one as a goal)

☐ Climb a Big Mountain	☐ Be More Confident
☐ Be Better Organized	☐ Be a Better Brother, Sister, or Friend
☐ Get and Keep a Job	☐ Be More Focused
☐ Procrastinate Less	☐ Be in Good Physical Shape
☐ Write an Article for a Magazine or Write a Book	☐ Build Muscles
☐ Drive Across America	☐ Speak a Different Language Fluently
☐ Control My Behavior Better	☐ Other Goals, Dreams or Bucket List Items that are not listed above: _____
☐ Own My Own Business	☐ Other: _____
☐ Live in a Different Country (which one: _____)	☐ Other: _____
☐ Be Less Concerned About What Others Think of Me	☐ Other: _____
☐ Be a Rock Climber	☐ Other: _____
☐ Be an Inspiration to Others	☐ Other: _____

Goals and Dreams: Put a check to the left if this is a Goal or Dream for you	**Values:** Put a check to the left if this matters a lot to you
	☐ Being Healthy
☐ Graduate High School ☐ Graduate College	☐ Honesty
☐ Break a record (what record?: _____)	☐ Helping people ☐ at school ☐ at home ☐ in the community
☐ Be rich (wealthy)	☐ Being a good: ☐ Brother/Sister ☐ Friend ☐ Son/Daughter

☐ Get in better physical shape or build muscles	☐ Having a lot of money (rich; wealthy)
☐ Join the Military	☐ Being productive and focused
☐ Own a Car	☐ Being a leader
☐ Increase my reading speed	☐ Being liked
☐ Have better control of my emotions or my behavior	☐ Spending time with: ☐ Friends ☐ Family
☐ Be less concerned about what others think of me	☐ Freedom
☐ Be a professional musician (singer, guitar player, piano player,…)	☐ Participating in youth activities: ☐ Sports ☐ Religious groups ☐ Scouts ☐ Dance ☐ Other: _____
☐ Be better organized	☐ Learning new things (gaining knowledge, wisdom, intelligence)
☐ Travel across America or travel the world	☐ Taking care of my pet
☐ Get a paying job	☐ Having time alone (being by myself)
☐ Have Nicer Clothes	☐ Being noticed when I do something well
☐ Get Married	☐ Achieving in school (get good grades; learn a lot)
☐ Be a _____ (job or occupation)	☐ Peace
☐ Be more easy going	☐ Fairness
☐ Be more confident	☐ Listening to music
☐ Live in a different country (which one: _____)	☐ Reading books (for pleasure)
☐ Do something dangerous or adventurous (risk-taking)	☐ Watching TV
☐ Live independently (not with parents)	☐ Playing video games
☐ Have a role in a movie or TV Show	☐ Creativity (art; build things; thinking creatively)
☐ Be a father or mother	☐ Being well liked by: ☐ Peers ☐ Adults
☐ Speak a different language fluently	☐ Being clean and neat
☐ Be on a TV show or in a movie	☐ Being listened to (being understood by others)
☐ Other Goals/Dreams/Bucket List Items Not Listed Above: _____	☐ Humor or Laughing
	☐ Power
	☐ Other things that matter to me: _____

Appendix D
Values Assessment (Middle-High School)

What Matters to Me Checklist **(Middle-High School)**	**Name:**_____		
Item:	**Matters to me:**		
	Circle how much each item matters to you		
Spending time with family	A Lot	A Little	Not at All
Spending time with friends	A Lot	A Little	Not at All
Owning a Car	A Lot	A Little	Not at All
Time alone	A Lot	A Little	Not at All
Graduating High School	A Lot	A Little	Not at All
Graduating College	A Lot	A Little	Not at All
Participating in sports	A Lot	A Little	Not at All
Excelling academically	A Lot	A Little	Not at All
Being listened to	A Lot	A Little	Not at All
Participating in youth-group activities	A Lot	A Little	Not at All
Being better organized	A Lot	A Little	Not at All
Participating in spiritual or religious activities	A Lot	A Little	Not at All
Volunteering / Community Service or Helping people	A Lot	A Little	Not at All
Being a Leader	A Lot	A Little	Not at All
Texting friends	A Lot	A Little	Not at All
Music	A Lot	A Little	Not at All
Traveling across America or travel the world	A Lot	A Little	Not at All
Having Wealth or lot of Money (Being Rich)	A Lot	A Little	Not at All
Being on a TV show, in a movie, or in a viral video	A Lot	A Little	Not at All
Reading books or magazines	A Lot	A Little	Not at All

Joining the Military/ Service to Country	A Lot	A Little	Not at All
Being a Leader	A Lot	A Little	Not at All
Having a job	A Lot	A Little	Not at All
Playing video games/ Gaming	A Lot	A Little	Not at All
Having nice clothes	A Lot	A Little	Not at All
Talking on the phone to friends	A Lot	A Little	Not at All
Spending time online surfing	A Lot	A Little	Not at All
Being a good brother/sister	A Lot	A Little	Not at All
Being more confident or more assertive	A Lot	A Little	Not at All
Watching TV	A Lot	A Little	Not at All
Watching movies	A Lot	A Little	Not at All
Have better control of my emotions	A Lot	A Little	Not at All
Have better control of my behavior	A Lot	A Little	Not at All
Humor or Laughing	A Lot	A Little	Not at All
Learning new things	A Lot	A Little	Not at All
Doing something dangerous, adventurous, or risk-taking	A Lot	A Little	Not at All
Being in competitive activities	A Lot	A Little	Not at All
Having less stress or managing your stress better	A Lot	A Little	Not at All
Creativity *(being imaginative, innovative, coming up with ideas)*	A Lot	A Little	Not at All
Friendship	A Lot	A Little	Not at All
Being a good friend	A Lot	A Little	Not at All
Getting in better physical shape or build muscles	A Lot	A Little	Not at All
Getting married someday	A Lot	A Little	Not at All

Improving the world	A Lot	A Little	Not at All
Honesty	A Lot	A Little	Not at All
Being clean and neat	A Lot	A Little	Not at All
Wisdom, Intelligence or knowledge	A Lot	A Little	Not at All
Taking care of my pet	A Lot	A Little	Not at All
Leisure time (fun or relaxation)	A Lot	A Little	Not at All
Creativity (art; writing; building things; thinking creatively)	A Lot	A Little	Not at All
Being well-liked by others	A Lot	A Little	Not at All
Power	A Lot	A Little	Not at All
Courage	A Lot	A Little	Not at All
Being a parent	A Lot	A Little	Not at All
Freedom	A Lot	A Little	Not at All
Being less concerned about what others think of me	A Lot	A Little	Not at All
Living independently (not with parents)	A Lot	A Little	Not at All
Being easy going about things (able to "go with the flow" when plans change)	A Lot	A Little	Not at All
Fairness or justice	A Lot	A Little	Not at All

Appendix E

Values Assessment (Elementary School)

What Matters to Me Checklist (Elementary)	Name:		
Item:	Matters to me:		
Spending time with my family	A Lot	A Little	Not at All
Playing with friends	A Lot	A Little	Not at All
Playing with my pet(s)	A Lot	A Little	Not at All
Taking care of my pet(s)	A Lot	A Little	Not at All
Spending time alone	A Lot	A Little	Not at All
Being noticed when I do something well	A Lot	A Little	Not at All
Peace	A Lot	A Little	Not at All
Having less stress in my life	A Lot	A Little	Not at All
Participating in sports or exercise	A Lot	A Little	Not at All
Participating in dance or cheerleading	A Lot	A Little	Not at All
Participating in scouts (cub scouts , brownies, girl scouts, boy scouts)	A Lot	A Little	Not at All
Getting good grades in school	A Lot	A Little	Not at All
Honesty	A Lot	A Little	Not at All
Being well-liked by my teachers	A Lot	A Little	Not at All
Being well-liked by my peers	A Lot	A Little	Not at All
Having a neat and clean room	A Lot	A Little	Not at All
Staying up late	A Lot	A Little	Not at All
Love	A Lot	A Little	Not at All
Cooking or Baking	A Lot	A Little	Not at All
Learning new things	A Lot	A Little	Not at All
Being listened to	A Lot	A Little	Not at All
Improving the world	A Lot	A Little	Not at All
Being smart	A Lot	A Little	Not at All
Going to church or synagogue (your place for worship)	A Lot	A Little	Not at All
Power	A Lot	A Little	Not at All
Texting friends or Talking to friends on the phone	A Lot	A Little	Not at All
Reading books or magazines	A Lot	A Little	Not at All
Being clean or neat	A Lot	A Little	Not at All
Music (listening to music; singing; playing an instrument)	A Lot	A Little	Not at All
Earning money (or having money)	A Lot	A Little	Not at All
Courage or Bravery	A Lot	A Little	Not at All
Eating healthy foods	A Lot	A Little	Not at All
Watching TV shows or Movies	A Lot	A Little	Not at All
Taking risks or doing dangerous things	A Lot	A Little	Not at All
Playing video games	A Lot	A Little	Not at All
Art (drawing; coloring; painting; clay,...)	A Lot	A Little	Not at All
Building things (Legos; models; Lincoln Logs,...)	A Lot	A Little	Not at All
Learning new things	A Lot	A Little	Not at All
Feeling Happy	A Lot	A Little	Not at All
Helping others	A Lot	A Little	Not at All
Fairness	A Lot	A Little	Not at All
Humor or Laughing	A Lot	A Little	Not at All
Other thing that really matters to me:_____	A Lot	A Little	Not at All
Other thing that really matters to me:_____	A Lot	A Little	Not at All

Source: Mann, 2013.

Appendix F

Managing Stress for School Success: Self-Assessment Data Summary

Name: _____		
Goals, Dreams and Bucket-List Assessment Summary		
Goals, Dreams, Bucket-List Items that I will Probably Achieve	Goals, Dreams, Bucket-List Items that I will Possibly Achieve	Goals, Dreams, Bucket-List Items that I am Unlikely to Achieve
From "What Matters?" Checklist: Items that Matter a lot to You (High Value)		
From Self-Descriptions Assessment (Optional)		
When You are with Family	When You are with Peers Outside of School	When You are in Class

Self-Description Assessment

(Adapted by Mann, 2013 from *Rush Neurobehavioral Center, Skokie, Illinois*)

3 adjectives that describe me...

When I am with my family:	When I am with peers outside of school:	When I am in class:
•	•	•
•	•	•
•	•	•

ADJECTIVES

Cheerful	Smart	Kind
Angry/Aggravated	Not smart	Mean
Gloomy, sad or depressed	Smart, but not 'book smart'	Real
Anxious, stressed out, or worried	Spaced out	Phony
Variable moods (ups and downs)	Confused	Talkative
Calm or comfortable	Impulsive (I act without thinking)	Shy
Easy-going	Thoughtful (I think before acting)	Isolated
Difficult to get along with	Aggressive	Cool
Quick-tempered (easily angered or frustrated)	Passive/Sluggish	Different
	Active/Energetic	Confident
Optimistic (positive and hopeful)	Quiet	Modest
Pessimistic (negative)	Loud	Arrogant or Cocky
Extroverted (outgoing; talkative)	Friendly	Insecure
Introverted (quiet; keep to self)	Unfriendly	Independent/Self-reliant

References

Ahuja, M. (13 March, 2013). Teens are spending more time consuming media, on mobile devices. *Washington Post Live*. Retrieved from www.washingtonpost.com/postlive/teens-are-spending-more-time-consuming-media-on-mobile-devices/2013/03/12/309bb242-8689-11e2-98a3-b3db6b9ac586_story.html.

Albrecht, K. (1979). *Stress and the manager*. New York: Touchstone Books.

APA (American Psychological Association). (2012). *Missing the health care connection*. Retrieved from www.apa.org/news/press/releases/stress/2012/full-report.pdf.

APA (American Psychological Association). (2013). *Diagnostic and statistical manual of mental disorders*. Fifth edition. Washington, DC: American Psychiatric Publishing.

APA (American Psychological Association). (2015). Children and trauma. Retrieved from www.apa.org/pi/families/resources/children-trauma-update.aspx.

APA (American Psychological Association). (n.d.). The different kinds of stress. Retrieved from www.apa.org/helpcenter/stress-kinds.aspx.

Achenbach, T. (1991). *Manual for the child behavior checklist/4–18 and 1991 profile*. Burlington, VT: University of Vermont Department of Psychiatry.

Beck, A. T. (1976). *Cognitive therapies and emotional disorders*. New York: New American Library.

Bernstein, J. (2009). *Liking the child you love*. Boston: Da Capo Lifelong Books.

Birmaher, B., Kaufman, J., Brent, D. A., Dahl, R. E., Perel, J. M., and Al-Shabbout, M. (1998). Neuroendocrine response to 5 hydroxyl-tryptophan in pre-pubertal children at risk of major depressive disorders. *Archives of General Psychiatry, 54*, 1113–1119.

Brown, E. J., McQuaid, J., Farina, L., Ali, R., and Winnick-Gelles, A. (2006). Matching interventions to children's mental health needs: Feasibility and acceptability of a pilot school-based trauma intervention program. *Education and Treatment of Children, 29*(2), 257–286.

Buchler, R. K. (2013). *Anxiety-reducing strategies in the classroom*. Doctoral dissertation, Western Michigan University. Retrieved from http://scholarworks.wmich.edu/cgi/viewcontent.cgi?article=1182&context=dissertations.

Chapman S. (2009). Mental health and smoking redux. *Australian & New Zealand Journal of Psychiatry*, 43, 579–580.

Chen, J. A., Berliner, L., and March, J. S. (2000). Treatment of children and adolescents. In E. B. Foa, T. M. Keane, and M. J. Friedman (Eds.), *Effective treatments for PTSD: Practical guidelines from the international society for traumatic stress studies* (213–216). New York: Guilford Press.

Cooley, M. (2007). *Teaching kids with mental health and learning disorders in the regular classroom*. Minneapolis, MN: Free Spirit Publishing.

Denham, T. E. (1990). Stress management: 3 simple movements. Retrieved from http://www.tomdenham.com/stress-management/.

Eichenbaum, H., and Cohen, N. J. (2001). *From conditioning to conscious recollection: Memory systems of the brain*. New York: Oxford University Press.

Felitti, V. J., Anda, R. F., Nordenberg, N., Williamson, D. F., Spitz, A. M., Edwards, V., Koss, M. P., and Marks, J. S. (1997). Relationship of childhood abuse and household dysfunction to many of the leading causes of death in adults. *American Journal of Preventative Medicine*, 14(4), 245–258. doi:10.1016/S0749-3797(98)00017-8.

Floren, G. (20 May, 2000). Review of the book *The courage to teach: Exploring the inner landscape of a teacher's life* by P. Palmer. Retrieved from http://www.mira-costa.cc.ca.us/home/gfloren/palmer.htm.

Fremont, W. (2003). School refusal in children and adolescents. *American Family Physician*, 68, 55–60.

Gordon, Whitson. (13 April, 2013). Top 10 instant stress busters. Retrieved from http://lifehacker.com/5994585/top-10-instant-stress-busters.

Gotzsche, P. (2014). Psychiatric drugs are doing us more harm than good. Retrieved from http://www.theguardian.com/commentisfree/2014/apr/30/psychiatric-drugs-harm-than-good-ssri-antidepressants-benzodiazepines.

Gregoire, C. (11 February, 2014). American teens are even more stressed than adults. *Huntington Post*. Retrieved from http://www.huffingtonpost.com/2014/02/11/american-teens-are-even-m_n_4768204.html.

Grohol, J. (2015). 15 common cognitive distortions. Retrieved from http://psychcentral.com/lib/15-common-cognitive-distortions/0002153.

Hasler, N. (2011). Mental illness in children. Retrieved from http://justthink.org/about/mental-illness-and-children/?gclid=CNSb0cHN8bgCFSdk7AodIx8A5w.

Heath, E. (13 February, 2013). Dealing with grief: Five things not to say and five things to say in a trauma involving children. Retrieved from http://www.huffingtonpost.com/rev-emily-c-heath/dealing-with-grief-five-t_b_2303910.html.

Heldt, E., Bochi, D. B., Margis, R., De Sousa, M. B., and Tonello, J. F. (2003). Cognitive behavioral group therapy in obsessive-compulsive disorders: A random clinical trial. *Psychotherapy and Psychosomatics*, 72, 211–216.

Jongsma, A. E., Peterson, M., and McInnes, W. P. (1996). *The child and adolescent psychotherapy treatment planner*. New York: John Wiley & Sons Inc.

Knight, R. T., Scabini, D., and Grabowecky, M. (1995). Role of human prefrontal cortex in attention control. *Advances in Neurology*, 66. Retrieved from http://citeseerx.ist.psu.edu/showciting?cid=1759238.

Lazarus, R. S., and Folkman, S. (1984). *Stress, appraisal and coping*. New York: Springer.

Mansueto, C., Ninan, P., Rothbaum, B., and Reeve, E. (2001). Trichotillomania and its treatment in children and adolescents: A guide for clinicians. Retrieved from www.trich.org.

Maruish, M. (2004). *The use of psychological testing for treatment planning and outcomes assessment: Instruments for adults* (Volume 1). Denmark: Lawrence Erlbaum Associates.

Mash, E., and Wolfe, D. (2002). *Abnormal child psychology*. Belmont, CA: Wadsworth Publishers.

Mental Health America. (2000). What every child needs for good mental health. Retrieved from http://www.nmha.org/farcry/go/information/get-info/children-smentalhealth/what-every-child-needs-for-good-mental-health.

Miller, L. H., and Smith, A. D. (1993). The stress solution. Retrieved from http://www.apa.org/helpcenter/.

Mindtools. (2016). Using affirmations: Harnessing positive thinking. Retrieved from http://www.mindtools.com/pages/article/affirmations.htm.

Muris, P., Merckelbach, H., Ollendick, T., King, N., and Bogie, N. (2002). Three traditional and three new childhood anxiety questionnaires: their reliability and validity in a normal adolescent sample. *Behaviour Research and Therapy*, 40, 753–772.

National Association of Mental Health. (2013). Children's mental health fact sheet: Improving lives, avoiding tragedies. Retrieved from http://library.dbsapages.org/post.php?id=393.

National Association of School Psychologists. (2001). A national tragedy: Helping children cope. Retrieved from http://www.nasponline.org/resources/crisis_safety/terror_general.aspx.

National Center for Health Statistics. (2007). Child welfare, substance use disorders and dependency. Retrieved from https://www.ncsacw.samhsa.gov/resources/AnnotatedBiblio.aspx.

National Child Trauma Stress Network. (October 2008). Child trauma toolkit for educators. Retrieved from www.NCTSN.org.

National Institute of Mental Health. (2013). Recognizing mental health problems in children. Retrieved from http://www.nmha.org/farcry/go/information/getinfo/children-s-mental-health/recognizing-mental-health-problems-in-children.

O'Brien, J. G., and Ristuccia, J. M. (2007). Classroom strategies for students exposed to trauma. Retrieved from www.doe.mass.edu.

Par Report. (2013). Definitions and statistics of adolescent and child trauma. Retrieved from http://www.shrdocs.com/presentations/58638/index.html.

Perth Center for Clinical Interventions. Perfectionism in perspective. Retrieved from http://www.cci.health.wa.gov.au/resources/infopax.cfm?Info_ID=52.

Pearlin, L. I., Menaghan, E. G., Lieberman, M. A., and Mullan, J. T. (1981). The stress process. *Journal of Health and Social Behavior*, 22, 337–356.

Ramamoorfhy, S., and Myers-Walls, J. A. (n.d.). Talking to a child who has been abused. Retrieved from https://www.extension.purdue.edu/providerparent/Parent-Provider%20Relationships/Talking_Child_Been_Abused.htm.

Seligman, E. P., and Petersen, C. (2004). *Character strengths and virtues: A handbook and classification.* New York, NY: Oxford University Press.

Shahar, B. T. (2009). *The pursuit of perfect.* New York, NY: McGraw Hill Publishers.

Staicu, M. L., and Cutov, M. (2010). Anger and health risk behaviors. *Journal of Medicine and Life*, 3(4), 372–375. Retrieved from http://www.ncbi.nlm.nih.gov/pmc/articles/PMC3019061/.

Toffler, A. (1971). *Future Shock.* New York: Bantam Books.

US Department of Health and Human Services. (1999). Mental health: A report of the surgeon general. Retrieved from http://www.surgeongeneral.gov/library/reports/index.html.

Vaalamo, I., Pulkkinen, L., Kinnunen, T., Kaprio, J., and Rose, R. J. (2002). Interactive effects of internalizing and externalizing problem behaviors on recurrent pain in children. *Journal of Pediatric Psychology*, 27(3), 245–257.

Vassar, G. (2011). The prevalence of trauma in children and teenagers. Retrieved from http://lakesideconnect.com/trauma-and-trauma-informed-care/the-prevalence-of-traumain-children-and-teenagers/.

Wagner, A. D. (2005). *Worried no more: Help and hope for anxious children.* Rochester, NY: Lighthouse Press.

Walkup, J. T., Albano, A. M., and Piacentinit, J. (2008). Cognitive behavioral therapy sertraline or a combination in childhood anxiety. *New England Journal of Medicine*, 359, 2757–2766.

WebMD (with The Cleveland Clinic). (2014). *Mental illness in children.* Retrieved from http://www.webmd.com/mental-health/mental-illness-children.

About the Authors

Marcel Lebrun is a professor at Plymouth State University in New Hampshire. He has thirty-six years of experience in education. He has published twelve books, numerous articles, and presented throughout the world on issues in special education, ethical leadership and advocacy, social justice, and mental health issues in students.

He has traveled extensively and visited eighty-seven countries worldwide. His quest is to bring awareness and strategies of mental health issues to the school system as well as in society. It is only in building awareness that we can empower adults and educators to give children a different experience than what they would normally get. Change can happen and will happen if we become advocates to empower all students worldwide.

Eric Mann, MSW, NH Center for Effective Behavioral Interventions and Supports (NH CEBIS) at SERESC, Inc. He is an education and behavioral consultant with thirty years of experience in public education and in private practice. He has worked as a teacher and counselor of children with emotional and learning challenges, as a psychotherapist for adults, couples, and families, and as a special education administrator. From 2002 to 2008, Eric co-directed a statewide *Positive Behavioral Interventions and Supports* initiative (PBIS-NH), and from 2007 to the present, he has co-directed three *Mental Health and Schools* initiatives. He has been a senior trainer in *Life space Crisis Intervention* (LSCI) since 2007 and has provided *Multi-Tiered Systems* training and coaching support to more than 300 schools since 2002.